CAMBRIDGE URBAN AND ARCHITECTURAL STUDIES

11 MODERN COUNTRY HOMES IN ENGLAND
    The Arts and Crafts Architecture of
    BARRY PARKER

T0381641

CAMBRIDGE URBAN AND ARCHITECTURAL STUDIES

General Editors

LESLIE MARTIN
Emeritus Professor of Architecture, University of Cambridge

LIONEL MARCH
Professor, Graduate School of Architecture and Urban Planning, University of California at Los Angeles

VOLUMES IN THIS SERIES

MODERN COUNTRY HOMES IN ENGLAND

The Arts and Crafts Architecture of
BARRY PARKER

Edited and introduced by
DEAN HAWKES

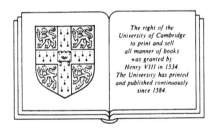

The right of the
University of Cambridge
to print and sell
all manner of books
was granted by
Henry VIII in 1534.
The University has printed
and published continuously
since 1584.

CAMBRIDGE UNIVERSITY PRESS

CAMBRIDGE
LONDON   NEW YORK   NEW ROCHELLE
MELBOURNE   SYDNEY

CAMBRIDGE UNIVERSITY PRESS
Cambridge, New York, Melbourne, Madrid, Cape Town, Singapore,
São Paulo, Delhi, Dubai, Tokyo

Cambridge University Press
The Edinburgh Building, Cambridge CB2 8RU, UK

Published in the United States of America by Cambridge University Press, New York

www.cambridge.org
Information on this title: www.cambridge.org/9780521136822

© Cambridge University Press 1986

This publication is in copyright. Subject to statutory exception
and to the provisions of relevant collective licensing agreements,
no reproduction of any part may take place without the written
permission of Cambridge University Press.

First published 1986
This digitally printed version 2010

A catalogue record for this publication is available from the British Library

Library of Congress Cataloguing in Publication data

Parker, Barry, 1867–1947.
Modern country homes in England: the arts and
crafts architecture of Barry Parker
(Cambridge urban and architectural studies: 11)
Bibliography: p.
Includes index.
1. Parker, Barry, 1867–1947. 2. Country homes –
England. 3. Arts and crafts movement – England –
Influence. I. Hawkes, Dean. II. Title. III. Series:
Cambridge urban and architectural studies; no. 11.
NA997.P35A4 1986 728.3′7′0924 85–29946

ISBN 978-0-521-24231-8 Hardback
ISBN 978-0-521-13682-2 Paperback

Cambridge University Press has no responsibility for the persistence or
accuracy of URLs for external or third-party internet websites referred to in
this publication, and does not guarantee that any content on such websites is,
or will remain, accurate or appropriate.

Contents

Illustrations

Acknowledgements

I wish to acknowledge the generous help I have received from many people in the production of this book. First amongst these are Peter Field and Doreen Cadwallader of the Letchworth Museum and the First Garden City Museum at Letchworth, who have, for many years, allowed me access to their collection of Barry Parker's papers and drawings. Dean Gerald McCue and Professor Henry Cobb of the Graduate School of Design at Harvard University helped me to travel to America to work on *The Craftsman* and contemporary American journals at the Loeb Library and the New England Deposit Library at Cambridge, Massachusetts. In Cambridge, England, I have benefited over the years from conversations with my colleagues Nicholas Bullock and David Handlin (now at Harvard), and from the work of all of the students in the Department of Architecture who have written dissertations on Arts and Crafts and Garden City topics. I should also like to thank the many present owners of Parker and Unwin's houses who have, without exception, allowed me access to their homes.

The majority of the illustrations in the book are reproduced from original drawings and photographs held at the First Garden City Museum at Letchworth. These are 1, 2, 3, 7, 8, 10, 13, 14, 18, 19, 20, 21, 23, 24, 25, 26, 27, 29, 30, 32, 34, 36, 37, 39, 43, 44, 45, 48, 49, 52, 53, 54, 58, 64, 65, 66, 67, 68, 69, 70, 71, 81, 86, 90, 91, 93, 95, 96, 97, 99, 104. Illustrations 5, 17, and 22 are reproduced from Parker and Unwin's collection of essays *The Art of Building a Home* published in 1901 by Longmans, Green and Co. Illustration 11 is from Raymond Unwin's *Town Planning in Practice*, published in 1909 by T. Fisher Unwin. Illustration 4 is from a drawing in the collection of the British Architectural Library's Drawings Collection. Illustrations 51 and 55 are modern photographs by the author and all other illustrations are redrawn by the author from the drawings which illustrated Parker's essays as they first appeared in *The Craftsman*

Cambridge, 1985   DEAN HAWKES

Introduction

The indulgent reader is asked to bear in mind that the following chapters appeared in substance first, under the title of 'Modern Country Homes in England', as a series of papers in the New York monthly, 'The Craftsman', with the willing concurrence of the Editor of which magazine this collected English edition has been prepared.

Of many shortcomings no one can be more conscious than the Author. Written in the scanty leisure of a busy man, often hastily, and at intervals spread over some two years, the papers were free from neither repetition nor discursiveness, nor was any strictly logical development of idea pursued; with some revision and compression they are now offered, modestly, for what they may be worth; not by any means as a literary exercise, but as the mature expression of the faith that guides in his work a sincere and experienced artist.

These words were written by Barry Parker in 1912. Unfortunately the book to which they were to be the Preface was not published. His English contemporaries were thus deprived of the opportunity of reading the ideas which he had set down for the American readers of *The Craftsman*.[1] The present book is a revival of Parker's project. The

1 Barry Parker, *c.* 1900

1

aim is to make an important document of the Arts and Crafts movement available to a wide readership. Because Parker chose to illustrate his essays entirely with buildings designed by himself and his partner Raymond Unwin, this is also an opportunity to assess their achievement as architects. This aspect of their work has, surprisingly, been largely neglected by historians of the period, perhaps because it was overshadowed by their work as the planners of the Garden City, or maybe because, for some, the Garden City connection automatically disqualified them from consideration as 'pioneers' of the modern movement.[2]

The body of Part Two is based upon Barry Parker's original text. This has been edited further to eliminate the repetition and discursiveness for which he apologised in his Preface, and the opportunity has been taken to place both the text and the buildings which it describes in their contemporary context and to discuss their qualities and value from a late twentieth-century viewpoint. Many of the illustrations are taken from the archive of original drawings and photographs held at the First Garden City Museum at Letchworth.

Part One

The Arts and Crafts Architecture of Barry Parker

A Biographical Sketch

The decade which began in 1860 saw the births of numerous men who were to have a profound influence upon the future direction of the art of architecture. On the continent the list includes Victor Horta (1861–1947), Theodor Fischer (1862–1938), Henri Van de Velde (1863–1957), Hector Guimard (1867–1947), J. M. Olbrich (1867–1908) and Peter Behrens (1868–1940). In America the major figure is without doubt Frank Lloyd Wright – whichever of the suggested birthdates is accepted – (1867(9)–1959),[1] and amongst others are Bernard Maybeck (1862–1957) and the Greene brothers, Henry M. (1867–1954) and Charles S. (1868–1957). At the turn of the century British domestic architecture received worldwide admiration and most of these buildings were the work of men of this generation. Amongst these Edgar Wood (1860–1935) practised mainly in the north of England, in and around Manchester, and C. R. Ashbee (1863–1942) was the man who perhaps gave Arts and Crafts ideals their most overt social expression when in 1902 he led the Guild of Handicraft away from London to establish a community at Chipping Camden in the Cotswolds.[2] M. H. Baillie Scott (1865–1945) is one of the most widely acknowledged of English architects of this period, his work receiving wide publicity both at home in Britain and on the continent.[3] Charles Rennie Mackintosh (1868–1928) and Edwin Lutyens (1869–1944),[4] although quite different in most respects, were in most assessments, the giants of the period.

Richard Barry Parker qualifies for membership of this impressive gathering, by having been born in 1867 at Chesterfield, an industrial town on the edge of the beautiful Derbyshire Peak District and, a more important measure, by the quality of his work. He attended the South Kensington Art School in London in 1886 and studied interior design with T. C. Simmonds at Derby in 1887–9. He then moved to Manchester where he served articles with G. Faulkner Armitage until 1893. He then went to live near Chesterfield with his elder sister, Ethel, and her husband – and half cousin – Raymond Unwin. Here he began his independent architectural career. In 1895 he moved across Derbyshire to Buxton in order to be near his ageing parents. The following year the Unwins came to join him and thus began an architectural partnership which was to last for eighteen years until

2 Family group at Buxton,
c. 1898. Barry Parker is
standing at the right,
Raymond Unwin is at the
left and Ethel Unwin (née
Parker) is seated front right.

Unwin moved, in 1914, into public service in the post of Chief
Inspector of Town Planning at the Local Government Board.

Unwin was four years older than Parker and although he was also
born in the industrial north at Rotherham in South Yorkshire he had
grown up in Oxford where his father taught at Balliol College School.
He returned to the north, however, in 1882 when he became an
apprentice engineer at the Staveley Coal and Iron Company near
Chesterfield. Here he eventually became responsible for the design of
cottages for the miners and in 1893 his architectural experience was
extended when he was asked to design the church in the village of
Barrow Hill outside Chesterfield. This coincided with Parker's arrival
and many years later Parker recalled this episode in their lives,
sketching an impression of youthful Arts and Crafts idealism, when
he wrote, 'Evening after evening, Unwin sat placing the little glass
cubes [for the mosaic reredos] in position on the cartoon which I had
made, in readiness for their transfer to the cement-rendered east wall
of the church, while I drew and his wife, my sister, read to us.'[5] It is
clear that there was a very close bond between the two men even
though the partnership between them was never formally sealed.
Many years later, looking back, Parker described it in romantic terms:
'When the partnership between him and me began no one can say.
We acted on the assumption that it would come into being before it
did. No partnership deed was ever drawn up. None was needed.
Mutual understanding was complete.'[6]

The practice began, as so many do, with commissions from family
and friends, and quickly flourished. Both men were committed to
improving the quality of working-class housing, and their first-hand

experience of conditions in the industrial towns would have had a persuasive influence upon them. They were actively involved in the socialist cause and were early members of the Fabian Society. It was almost inevitable that they would become steeped in the ideas of William Morris, and Unwin, who seemed to be the more overtly political of the two, travelled around the industrial towns addressing branches of 'The Labour Church', on such subjects as 'The Life and Work of William Morris'.

All of this predisposed them towards giving expression to Morris's visions through their work and in 1901 they collected together a series of lectures and essays under the title of *The Art of Building a Home*.[7] The titles of some of these pieces indicate the Arts and Crafts roots of their thinking. Parker wrote 'Of the Dignity of All True Art' and Unwin 'Of Art and Simplicity'. The social dimension of their interests is reflected in other titles, 'Of the Smaller Middle Class House', 'Of the Art of Designing Smaller Houses and Cottages' and 'Of Co-Operation in Building'.

These themes were illustrated by their own designs, and the book, which ran to a second edition in the year of its publication, must have brought them to the attention of new clients. In 1902 Joseph and Seebohm Rowntree, of the Quaker chocolate-making family, appointed Parker and Unwin as architects for the model village of New Earswick near York. Here they were able to give large-scale expression to their ideas and to gain the experience which equipped them to succeed in the limited competition, held in the following year, for the design of the First Garden City at Letchworth in Hertfordshire under the direct inspiration of Ebenezer Howard. The other competitors were W. R. Lethaby and Halsey Ricardo, who decided to submit a joint proposal, and Geoffrey Lucas and Sidney Cranfield.

By winning this competition Parker and Unwin were thrust more prominently into the public eye and their practice grew rapidly. Of perhaps equal importance for the development of their careers was the fact that they were compelled by the size of the task to open an office in the southern counties. The design for the Garden City was prepared, in a cottage on the site, by Unwin assisted by Robert Bennett who was an articled pupil in the office. These two were visited by Parker as often as the demands of the Buxton office would allow. After their appointment as Consulting Architects to First Garden City Limited they rented offices at Baldock, the nearest town, and soon leased a site in Letchworth on which to build an office (see also plan, Ill. 92).[8]

Nearby, Unwin built a house for himself and his family (see Ills. 44 and 45), but very shortly, in 1906, he was invited, by Dame Henrietta Barnett, to make a plan for Hampstead Garden Suburb. He moved to live at Wyldes, North End, Hampstead, a beautiful old house, intending to return to Letchworth after some two years. In the event

3 Interior of the drawing
office at Letchworth, *c.*1908

the attractions of both the house and life on the fringe of the capital
proved too great and the practice was, for the remaining years to
1914, based upon the two offices: Letchworth, with Parker in charge,
and Hampstead under Unwin.

All of the evidence suggests that this separation did not break the
bond of spirit between the two men, even though their interests
began to move in different directions. The Hampstead office
concentrated on work in the Garden Suburb and attracted many men
who were to make their mark elsewhere. In international terms the
most notable of these was Ernst May who was to become
'Stadtbaurat' (City Architect) of Frankfurt in 1925. There he was
responsible for numerous housing projects which, beneath their
modern movement clothing, reveal many qualities which bear
witness to the influence of his association with Parker and Unwin.[9] In
Letchworth there was much to be done in the Garden City, both in
designing new housing schemes for the various cottage societies,
which were building low-cost dwellings, and in commissions for
larger houses nearby and much further afield.

An additional responsibility which Parker and Unwin assumed was
that of drafting and administering the Building Regulations for First
Garden City Limited. These went beyond the provisions of conven-

tional building bye-laws in force in England at the time in imposing restrictions on the density at which houses could be built. This ranged from a maximum of twelve to the acre for houses costing less than £200, to four to the acre for lavish designs costing £500 or upwards. Other concerns were with the quality of construction and design of the dwellings themselves.[10] The administration of these regulations must have itself been time-consuming. It is interesting to discover contemporaries as notable as Baillie Scott being subjected to the scrutiny of Parker and Unwin in gaining approval for their designs in Letchworth.[11] It was by these means that the essential qualities that distinguish the Garden City from most contemporary housing in England were achieved and maintained.

Against this background of intensive activity both partners continued to produce written statements about their ideals and commitments. In 1909 Unwin's increasing interest in the cause of town planning was given full expression with the publication of his book *Town Planning in Practice*.[12] This coincided with the passing of the Town Planning Act of 1909, and Unwin, who regularly revealed a shrewd sense of timing, wrote, surely with false modesty, in his Preface:

When a Bill conferring town planning powers on municipal bodies was promised by the Government, it occurred to me that it would probably be of use, if some of the maps, photographs and other material which I had collected during some years' study and practice of what I have ventured to call the art of town planning could be put together and published. Hence this book. The spare time at my disposal has only enabled me to deal in an introductory and imperfect manner with the different points raised. . . .

This 'modest' effort is a work of over 400 pages in length with over 300 illustrations! Its influence in shaping the development of towns and cities is evident throughout Britain, where, to this day, most housing development is conceived in terms of ideas which were first given expression in the Garden City – although, alas, seldom now with the sensitivity and flair which characterised the original models. The overseas influence of the book may be less explicit, but was nonetheless far-reaching, as much for the analysis which is recommended as for the forms and images which it contains.

Parker's essays in *The Craftsman* add up to a body of work almost as substantial as *Town Planning in Practice* and it is perhaps not too fanciful to suggest that he saw them as a complement to Unwin's book. In terms of scale they begin where Unwin stopped, taking us from consideration of site layout, down through garden design, to the smallest details of the individual house. Walter Creese has written with great insight that,

The particular message of Parker and Unwin's architecture seems to be that British [town] planning, as we know it, arose as much out of William Morris's

Arts and Crafts as out of any independent thought about cities alone. The houses of Parker and Unwin are a visible link between the crafts of Parker and Unwin and the towns they created.[13]

The invitation from Gustav Stickley, the owner and editor of *The Craftsman*, to write at such length in his journal must have been seized by Parker as an ideal opportunity to re-affirm the scope of his and Unwin's architectural vision as it had been first presented in *The Art of Building a Home*, and had subsequently been applied and tested in their practice.

Gustav Stickley, *The Craftsman* and England

Gustav Stickley (1857–1942) was born in Wisconsin, the son of a stonemason.[1] While he was still in his teens he discovered the writings of John Ruskin. These were to remain a lifelong influence and directed his attention towards events and personalities in England. In 1900 he opened a factory at Eastwood, New York, to manufacture Arts and Crafts style furniture. The following year he began publication of *The Craftsman*.[2] This quickly became an important influence on architectural ideas and public taste in America. In May 1903 Stickley published the first of many designs for *Craftsman Homes*, which was his own work, assisted by E. G. W. Dietrich. Kornwolf has pointed to the similarity between this house and aspects of Baillie Scott's work, but Stickley himself saw his ideal in the work of Parker and Unwin. In reviewing *The Art of Building a Home* he wrote:

... two well-known English architects, Barry Parker and Raymond Unwin, who in a series of lectures published under the title of 'The Art of Building a Home' have entered a plea for greater honesty in architecture and greater sincerity in decoration which ought to strike a responsive chord in the heart of every American who has contemplated the foolish, unthinking, artificial structures which we have vainly called homes.

In the introduction to this valuable little book Messrs. Parker and Unwin take up the question of lack of thought in architecture in so simple, straightforward and illuminating a fashion that it has seemed wise to present it to the readers of *Craftsman Homes* as expressing our needs and more fully our own ideals![3]

Stickley's passion for things English is demonstrated by the sheer number of references to English sources which appeared consistently through the magazine. Epigrammatic quotations from Ruskin frequently appear and, as late as 1915,[4] the entire editorial was given over to an extended Ruskin quotation which Stickley prefaced by writing:

For the architectural number of 'The Craftsman' surely no introduction can be more fitting than the following words by one of the world's greatest philosophers and writers upon this important theme. For in them we find expressed our own point of view not only about architecture but about life.

11

Another favourite of Stickley's was Edward Carpenter, who was quoted almost as frequently as was Ruskin, and whose chapter, 'A Simplification of Life' from *England's Ideal* was printed as the introduction to the second edition of *Craftsman Homes* in 1909.[5] Coincidentally, Carpenter was a friend of Parker and Unwin, and Unwin's son, Edward, was named after him.

English architects whose work was illustrated or mentioned include Edgar Wood, Edwin Lutyens, Halsey Ricardo, Ernest Newton, C. F. A. Voysey, M. H. Baillie Scott and George Walton. The last four of these were quoted in an article 'The Modern House Beautiful – An Exhortation' by Antoinette Rehmann which appeared in 1905 and was almost certainly inspired by the publication of Muthesius's *Das Englische Haus*.[6] Voysey received special attention twice. In 1911 an extended article on his furniture design[7] was illustrated by exterior views of a number of his houses and by interiors of 'Holly Mount', at Beaconsfield, 'Littleholme' near Kendal and 'The Homestead' at Frinton-on-Sea. The following year, in the issue after the publication of the last of Barry Parker's essays, Voysey himself wrote a passionate manifesto on 'The Quality of Fitness in Architecture and Furniture'.[8] A flavour of this powerful piece is conveyed by his declaration that 'Fitness is a divine law, and by fitness we mean not only *material suitability, but moral fitness – that* which expresses our best thoughts and feelings, and our purest moral sense. We must recoil from all forms of dishonesty.'

The European avant-garde was almost entirely disregarded by Stickley, but in 1912 attention was given to H. P. Berlage in two essays.[9] The first of these, unsigned, almost certainly by Stickley, and the second by W. A. Purcell (1880–1965) and George G. Elmslie (1871–1952). These men were important members of the Chicago school of architecture which grew up around Louis Sullivan and Frank Lloyd Wright, Elmslie having worked in Sullivan's office for nearly twenty years before forming a partnership with Purcell in 1909.[10] The second of these essays appeared in the same issue of the magazine as an article about Gaudi's Sagrada Familia Cathedral in Barcelona.[11]

It is surprising that Frank Lloyd Wright's work was never published by Stickley. Louis Sullivan published four essays in 1906 called 'What is Architecture – A Study of the American People',[12] and his bank at Owatonna, Minnesota, was illustrated in 1908.[13] At about this time the work of Greene and Greene was extensively described by Stickley,[14] and later Irving Gill featured in a number of articles.[15]

Both Parker and Unwin appeared early in the life of *The Craftsman*. In 1902 Parker wrote on 'Beauty in Buildings and Some Things that Lead to It':[16]

... to regard architecture as something which may be separated from the art of building is to take a false position, and one which will set us on a false tack at the very outset ... My intention is to try to formulate a few fundamental principles and guiding instincts which have led to beautiful results, and the neglect of which, on the other hand, has led to failure in all styles, and at all times, throughout the history of the art.

These sentiments being firmly in the mainstream of Arts and Crafts doctrine must have been irresistible to Stickley. In 1905 Raymond Unwin wrote on 'The Improvement of Towns',[17] in an issue which also published a design for a cushion cover by Parker 'worked by Miss Ada Henk'! Throughout the next volume,[18] the English influence was predominant, including extracts from Parker's essay 'Of Our Education in Art' from *The Art of Building a Home*, and Unwin contributed a postscript on 'The Life of Design'. Edward Carpenter was quoted at some length and there was a report on the Cheap Cottages Exhibition held at Letchworth in 1905 in which, amongst others, were illustrated Baillie Scott's design for Elmwood Cottages and Geoffrey Lucas's pretty houses in Paddock Close.

In January 1910 two articles appeared about Parker and Unwin's work. The first[19] was an extended review of *Town Planning in Practice*.

This book was published in England only two months ago and is not as yet to be obtained in America, but being largely the record of actual experience, we quote from it as having great practical value to all in this country who are interested in the planning of new towns, villages and suburbs and in the remodelling of those already in existence.

The other essay, on Parker,[20] introduced him in enthusiastic terms. It concluded that

The principles that use and fitness alone must rule the planning and construction of all buildings, and that each building must be designed as a whole and that design carried out consistently down to the last detail of furnishing, are the mainsprings of action in all his work and furnish the reason for the vitality and charm of everything he does.

The stage was thus set for Parker's series of articles, '. . . articles which will be found most suggestive both to architects and home builders'.

Material and Meaning in Arts and Crafts Theory

As has already been noted, these *Craftsman* essays complete the trilogy of Parker's and Unwin's major published works which began in 1901 with *The Art of Building a Home*, written jointly, and was advanced by Unwin's publication of *Town Planning in Practice* in 1909. As Parker explained in the introductory essay he saw them very much as a sequel to *The Art of Building a Home* and an opportunity to refine and re-affirm the beliefs expressed a decade earlier. The relationship with *Town Planning in Practice* rests upon the way in which shared principles are applied to the two different scales of activity, of planning towns and of designing the buildings which make up those towns. Walter Creese has pointed out the consistency of vision which unites all that Parker and Unwin did and his observation may be supported by making reference to their writings.

It is easy to demonstrate the connection between the two works at a technical level. Perhaps the most obvious example is to be found in their studies of the attractions of terraced as opposed to detached houses in layouts of the same density. Unwin's case, with his preoccupation with the large scale, remains a block diagram, whereas Parker shows the interior planning of the houses in detail (see Ills. 88 and 89). The point being made is, however, identical.

At a deeper level, we can discover a complete unity of thought in their attitude to architectural and social order, and to the relationship between them. Unwin wrote of cities: '. . . I feel very much convinced that town planning to be successful must be largely the outgrowth of the circumstances of the site and the requirements of the inhabitants',[1] and Parker spoke as follows of the design of a house:

With as complete a knowledge as he can get of the people for whose lives he is to create a home, and of their requirements and tastes, the designer must go on to the site and let it dictate to him what shall be the interior arrangement of the house, and largely what shall be its exterior treatment.

In these statements we can see the functionalist dimension of Arts and Crafts theory declared as the basis for action at all scales. This pragmatism plays a central role in Parker's and Unwin's thought. The street scenes which vividly illustrate *Town Planning in Practice* find their counterparts in the houses which Parker describes. Their

14

preferences clearly lean towards the vernacular tradition but they are at pains to show that this has a rational basis which can be discovered and thus applied in more self-conscious designs. They are not, however, dogmatic on questions such as the relation between formal and informal planning and composition. Unwin writes at length on the matter in a chapter 'Of Formal and Informal Beauty' and concludes that

. . . what is needed to guide the town planner is not so much strong prejudice in favour of either formal or informal treatment, but rather a right appreciation of the meaning and value of each, and a just estimate in each case as it arises of the reasons in favour of one or the other.[2]

Parker's approach to the matter is different, but, perhaps not surprisingly, he reaches similar conclusions.

We have an instinct that there is something inherently right in the symmetrical arrangement of buildings. This we find grows in strength as we strive after sensible arrangement; and symmetry so arrived at will probably have a feeling of inevitability unattainable where balance of parts has been regarded as of the first importance . . . In addition to an intuitive feeling for the symmetrical arrangement of buildings, we have an instinct for uniformity where it is logical and natural. The introduction of variety for its own sake would seem to be almost as dangerous as to try and fit planning to preconceived façades . . . We shall seldom, if ever, find such variety to have been a good exchange for the quiet and calm which might have resulted from uniformity.

This theme is continued when we come to matters of building construction, where we find Parker placing himself firmly in the centre of the Arts and Crafts tradition:

We saw there could be only one true way of going to work, and that was to build in the simplest and most direct way possible just that which would best fulfil the functions and meet the requirements in each instance, trusting solely to direct and straightforward construction, frankly acknowledged and shown, to produce beauty, instead of to decoration and ornament, pilasters, cornices, entablatures, pediments and what not, superimposed or added and hiding or disguising the constructional features.

A comparison with Baillie Scott on this subject shows an essential similarity of view: 'The house which, for want of a better word, we must continue to differentiate from the ordinary house as "artistic", bases its claims not on its frillings and on its adornments, but on the very essence of its structure'.[3] But *he* is more yielding on the question of decoration:

In its construction the exposure of every feature of the building is not necessarily involved, and though the structure indeed largely contributes to the beauty of the house, it is often obscured to meet practical requirements, or to supply surfaces for plain spaces of pure colour or thoughtfully conceived decoration.[4]

Voysey has already been quoted on the subject of *fitness*,[5] and later in the same essay he enlarged on the subject of form and construction.

To squeeze the requirements of a mansion into the semblance of a Grecian temple must involve the violation of fitness and the expression of false sentiment. We are not Greeks, nor have we a Grecian climate, or Grecian materials and conditions. Moreover, an attentive study of local material and conditions will greatly aid us in securing harmony and rhythm, making our building look as if it grew where it stood in loving co-operation with its immediate surroundings.

The knowledge of foreign architecture has done much to destroy the full and complete harmony in modern work which is the characteristic feature of all the finest buildings throughout the world. The more we study the conditions under which we build the better.

A frank use of common material well proportioned and fitly used, will often give a charming effect by reason of its frankness. You see at a glance what it is and feel taken into the architect's confidence; whereas the covering up of construction with cheap elaboration, or material made to imitate something more costly, only makes you feel you have been cheated.

. . . all ornament is pernicious unless it inspires good thought and feeling in others.

The roots of all these declarations clearly lie in the tradition which began with Ruskin and which Morris carried further later in the nineteenth century. Hermann Muthesius, who was sent to Britain by the German government, expressly to observe developments in domestic architecture, described with great perception the influence of Arts and Crafts theory on the work of these architects – that is the generation which began with Voysey and Lethaby, rather than the older men such as Shaw and Webb. He wrote of this younger group:

New aims now arose; by and large they were the ones proclaimed so vehemently by Ruskin and Morris, which concerned the qualities of material and labour. The idea began to take root that the value of a piece lay mainly in its execution, which must be technically correct and appropriate to the material and workmanship. All the prerequisites for every man-made object should lie in its material, purpose and construction, its form should be consequent upon these prerequisites and not upon an independent preconceived idea.[6]

The relationship between these principles and all of the mature architecture of men such as Voysey, Baillie Scott and Parker and Unwin is clear to see. What is interesting is to ask why Parker, writing in 1910, and Voysey in 1912, should both feel it necessary to make such strong statements, to *restate* their beliefs, which they had by then demonstrably applied to good effect. The answer to the question almost certainly lies in the changes in architectural taste which were occurring in England at this time.

The growth of the idea of a *profession* of architecture, which was gaining ground at the end of the nineteenth century,[7] was plainly antithetical to the doctrines of the Arts and Crafts. Lethaby objected in strong terms: 'The system of professionalism is an outcome of the vicious idea that the real business of a builder is not to build well – as mercifully many still do – but to cheat . . .' .[8] Woven into the fabric of the movement towards professionalism was a stylistic dimension in which the orderliness and discipline of the classical style had self-evident attractions to men who were anxious to demonstrate their respectability to clients who were, increasingly, to be found in the world of commerce. The combined forces of self-interested professionalism and the relevance of the classical manner to the design problems of the Edwardian period – banks, insurance offices, hotels and the like – all put pressure on the Arts and Crafts architects, who had built very few public and commercial buildings. It must be said that this probably had more to do with the apparently never ending flow of congenial domestic commissions which these architects received in the late 1890s and first years of the twentieth century, rather than any inherent shortcoming of their manner of building, which, as has been shown elsewhere, could be most successfully adapted to larger scale problems when required.[9]

The fact is, however, that as Robert Macleod has concluded,[10] 'The end result was, after 1910, a kind of stylistic truce. The derived Classicism held sway . . .'. This position must have been very difficult for the established Arts and Crafts architects to accept, particularly those who had committed their beliefs to print as vigorously as had Parker and Voysey. With their backs against the stylistic wall they must have found Stickley's continued advocacy of their ideals, and his ability to provide them with a platform in *The Craftsman*, quite irresistible.

In the event their efforts were in vain, the tide of taste was flowing too swiftly to be reversed, and in 1914 the classicists' cause was given powerful intellectual support with the publication of Geoffrey Scott's *The Architecture of Humanism*.[11] This book received widespread acclaim, probably more because it was well attuned to the prevailing mood than because it contained any eternal truths. Scott's argument is sophisticated and wide-ranging. His case for the universal validity of classicism was based upon a sustained, if coyly undeclared, critique of Ruskin and all he stood for and, by implication, therefore, of all those whose views and practices derived from him and his theories. It is easy to recognise some element of Arts and Crafts theory in each of Scott's 'Fallacies', the *Romantic*, the *Mechanical*, the *Ethical* and the *Biological*. In these the opposition between the two points of view could hardly have been expressed in more extreme terms.

A decade earlier Muthesius had drawn attention to an important omission from the statements of principle in the Arts and Crafts movement. This was the absence of what he described as the 'purely sentimental qualities, such as mood, poetry, rhythm, symbolism and fantasy . . . The movement that returned so wholeheartedly to ideals of pure craftsmanship may be described as a kind of material-ism . . .'.[12] Up to a certain point this analysis holds good; as we have already seen questions of fitness, purpose, material and workman-ship occupy a central place in Arts and Crafts theory, but one does not have to delve too deeply into the literature to discover evidence of a deep interest in matters of the heart as well as of the mind. Ruskin himself is absolutely emphatic in the Fourth Aphorism in *The Seven Lamps of Architecture*,[13] although it has to be acknowledged that his purpose is overtly moralistic: 'All architecture proposes an effect on the human mind, not merely a service to the human frame.' And Lethaby, in the introduction to his profound and still challenging book *Architecture, Mysticism and Myth*,[14] wrote 'Architecture . . . interpenetrates building not for satisfaction of the simple needs of the body, but for the complex ones of the intellect.' Voysey, in the essay on 'The Quality of Fitness', already quoted,[15] made an explicit statement about the deeper meanings of the forms and elements of his buildings: '. . . a careful study of our climate makes us emphasise our roofs to suggest protection from weather. Large, massive chimneys imply stability and repose. Long, low buildings also create a feeling of restfulness and spaciousness. Small windows in proportion to wall space suggest protection.' In his writings, Barry Parker, whilst not entirely ignoring appeals to Muthesius's 'sentimental qualities', is mainly concerned with practical formulae. But this should not be interpreted as evidence of a lack of concern for deeper qualities; this is amply demonstrated through the buildings which speak eloquently for themselves.

Parker and Unwin's Houses

There is a remarkable contrast between Parker and Unwin's early designs from the years 1896 to 1900, which were illustrated in *The Art of Building a Home*, and the mature work which forms the substance of *The Craftsman* essays. The early work was frequently inventive and individual, particularly in the design of the main rooms, and it is possible to detect characteristics which were to become hallmarks of the later houses. The main problem which confronted them was how to give lucid expression to the principles which they were beginning to define and it is very clear that the overt mediaevalism of these early houses, with half-timbering both inside and out, and heavy joinery details was an unsatisfactory medium for their purpose.

They were quick to learn, however, and the example of Voysey was clearly a major influence upon them, particularly in helping them to simplify and clarify their approach to the exterior of their buildings. 'The Homestead' at Chesterfield (1903) (see Ill. 13), the house Parker chose to illustrate the first of *The Craftsman* essays, shows the Voysey influence explicitly in the bay windows on the south façade, which are a thinly disguised borrowing from 'Broadleys' at Windermere (1898). It is unfortunate that, perhaps in trying to avoid an exact copy, Parker and Unwin adopted a less satisfactory relationship between roof and wall than Voysey and, by using only two bays instead of three, gave themselves a compositional problem in handling the empty centre of the façade which they failed to solve.

Most Arts and Crafts architects were sensitive to the desirability of a southerly orientation for the main rooms of a house. In *The Art of Building a Home*, Parker and Unwin had written, 'It is now generally realised that no sacrifice is too great which is necessary to enable us to bring plenty of sunshine into all main living rooms . . .'.[1] In 1906 Baillie Scott, in discussing 'The House in Relation to its Site', said '. . . the question of aspect will be the dominant factor in determining the situation of the house',[2] and Voysey, three years later, repeated the argument: 'Will it not . . . be better for soul and body to capture the early morning sun, which is never too hot in England, and is a great purifying influence . . .?'.[3]

The plan of 'The Homestead' (see Ill. 12) respects this principle to the letter, with all the main rooms facing south. The site is to the

19

4 'Broadleys' at Windermere, by C. F. A. Voysey, 1898

north of a road and the driveway is brought along the eastern boundary and around to an entry court at the north-east, at which point the functional differentiation between the main block of the house and the secondary wing containing the kitchen and the scullery is made clear. This is a device which was used by many Arts and Crafts architects, as reference to designs by Voysey, Baillie Scott, Mackintosh and many others will make clear.[4] 'The Homestead' serves to illustrate some of the characteristics which distinguish the houses of Parker and Unwin. Almost without exception the exteriors of their houses are straightforward, expressing their commitment 'to build in the simplest and most direct way possible'. But these simple façades conceal interiors which are rich and complex and are the more remarkable because they are unannounced from outside. In this case, the hall is an astonishing room.[5] It is based upon a major double-height volume, lit from the south by the Voyseyan semi-circular bay window. Opening off this are a series of smaller areas at both ground and first floor. The ingle-nook was always conceived by Parker and Unwin as the focus of family life in the winter months and was unfailingly designed and detailed with loving care. In this room we find two ingles. The larger one was meant for use when the whole family was present or for entertaining. Its use would be extravagant when just one or two were at home and so a two-seater is tucked under the stairs on the north wall. This has a summertime counterpart in the window seats which were placed next to it at the north-west corner of the room – just the right place to receive the last rays of the evening sun.

This play between spatial complexity and the poetic expression of function, contained by a simple enclosure, is a common theme in *The Craftsman* essays. The house at Caterham, for Mr Steers (see Ills. 23–5), shows how the idiosyncracies of an eccentric client, interested in Eastern martial arts, were exploited to good effect in both the sequence of spaces from the entrance to the living room and, particularly, in the replacement of the hall, with its usual associations with the romantic mediaevalism of, say, William Morris's *News from Nowhere*, by a gymnasium with implicit oriental connotations.

The Vause House at Rugby (see Ills. 38 and 39) is very different in scale and intention, but the trick is repeated. An apparently unassuming house on a typical, narrow suburban site is found to contain two ground floor rooms of great richness and beauty. The division between the living room and dining room is manipulated to form an ingle-nook and to frame the foot of the staircase. The two bay windows on the road front provide places in which to enjoy the evening sun and the south facing gable wall is inflected to allow a ray of morning light to enter through the ingle-nook.

Parker and Unwin's view of family life was a powerful influence upon their designs. Their socialist ideals made them reject the Victorian notion that children should be seen and not heard. They believed that the family should spend a good deal of time together and that the house should be conceived to allow this in all its aspects.

Let us have in our houses, rooms where there shall be space to carry on the business of life, freely and with pleasure, with furniture made for use; rooms where a drop of water spilled is not fatal; where the life of a child is not made a burden to it by unnecessary restraint; plain, simple and ungarnished if necessary, but honest.[6]

In all their houses, however large or small, the living room is a direct expression of this ideal. We have seen something of this at 'The Homestead' and the Vause House where one can imagine a busy, contented domestic scene with ease. In the Derbyshire days, Parker made a drawing which must have had a seminal influence on their work. This was a 'design for the living room in a house to have this room, sanctum, kitchens, offices and bedroom accommodation only'.[7]

There is the inevitable ingle-nook, a recess for study, everyday items such as crockery are conspicuously, but neatly, stored, the importance of music is symbolised by the provision of a pipe organ on the gallery, the visual arts are applied to the decoration of the walls – no easel pictures here! – and the central activity of dining rightly occupies the middle of the room. It is worth noting the way in which fixed furniture and the inner structure of the building are brought together with subtle interdependencies, in particular the conjunction of the stair and the ingle. Fitting a seat under the reduced headroom of the stair was a trick which they were to use over and over again.

5 Design for a living room
from *The Art of Building a
Home*

Underlying the planning of most of these rooms is a consistent
geometrical system. Each of them has a principal rectangular volume
which is elaborated by the addition of a series of smaller spaces,
usually associated with a specific function. In the house at
Northwood near Stoke-on-Trent this can be clearly seen in the design
of the living room (see Ills. 17 and 18). The central volume is clearly
defined by the picture rail which runs around its full perimeter. The
ingle-nook and the large bay window are the largest extensions of
this, and between them is a triangular alcove beneath an arched
opening which contains the piano, neatly forming a proscenium
frame for family music making. Two smaller extensions of the space
contain a small oriel window looking out onto the verandah and the
large, built-in sideboard.

Geometry was also used at a larger scale as an organising device in
the planning of entire houses. The clearest example of this is found in
'The Cottage' at Newton near Cambridge (see also Ills. 50 and 51).
The plan of this house is based on a rectangle subdivided into four
squares within which the main zones of the plan are disposed. This
simple diagram is adapted more precisely to the conditions of both the
programme for the house and of the site by the clever way in which
the entrance and the living room bay window are generated by
placing half-sized squares on the diagonal of the square at the south
end of the main block. A similar but more elaborate system was used

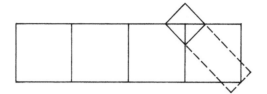

6 Plan analysis of 'The Cottage', Newton, near Cambridge

in an unexecuted project for 'A Country Cottage' with which it has a clear relationship.

A more subtle, but nonetheless equally strong, geometrical framework is used in 'Briarside', a small house at Letchworth (see Ills. 47 and 48). At first sight this house is deceptively similar to many of the suburban houses which were built in great numbers in English suburbs between the wars. Closer examination shows that its plan is based on a precise square, which is inflected and adjusted to produce an arrangement of the usual rooms, placing emphasis upon the main living room, and which contrives to place the ingle-nook and bay window in a clever relationship both to each other and to orientation. The roof which is then fitted onto this plan cleverly conceals the underlying simplicity.

A further variation on the geometrical theme comes in 'Little Molewood', a small house at Hertford (see Ills. 31 and 32). Here the plan is based upon two identical rectangles, one of which is given over entirely at the ground floor to the main living rooms, the other contains the entrance and the service rooms. As always the basic geometry is used as the starting point of the design and its presence is concealed from casual observation by a number of inflections and adjustments. In this case, these occur in the entrance hall and, particularly, in the arrangement of the main stair which occupies both rectangles, starting off opposite the entrance and turning back to return over the seat by the fireplace in the Hall.

We have already seen that Parker was attracted by the use of symmetry in buildings and was opposed to the gratuitous and arbitrary introduction of 'variety for its own sake'. But the formal symmetry of the classical language was clearly not for him. In many of his houses he achieved an effective reconciliation of these tastes. The façade of the principal wing of 'Little Molewood' is perfectly symmetrical, but the plan behind manages to achieve an unforced differentiation between the two rooms. The Vause House achieves a similar arrangement with its conjunction of a symmetrical street façade and free planning of the living room. An unexecuted project for a cottage near Rochdale for Mrs Ashworth has a plan based upon a bi-partite division of a simple rectangle, which is then made asymmetrical in its detailed planning with the entrance off-axis (see Ills. 56–8). The symmetry is restored, however, in the façade by the placement of a central gable which is almost a pediment.

The doctrine of simple, undecorated construction was fairly

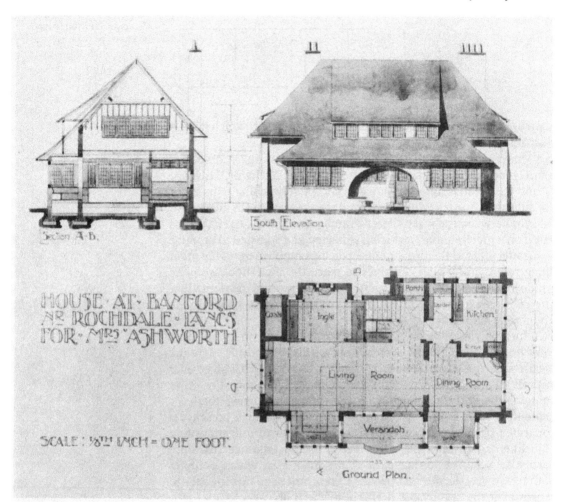

Section A·B.

South Elevation

HOUSE·AT·BAMFORD
NR·ROCHDALE·LANCS
FOR·MRS·ASHWORTH

SCALE : ⅛" INCH = ONE FOOT.

Porch
Kitchen
Cash
Ingle
Living   Room
Dining Room
Verandah
Ground Plan.

7 'Whirriestone', Rochdale:
first design, plan, section
and elevation

consistently respected in these houses, although plastered walls and
quite expensive floor finishes were often used. Two houses at
Letchworth probably stand closer to this ideal than any others. The
first of these is that built for Parker's painter brother, in which the
whitewashed walls, exposed structured timber and plain deal floor
boards are supplemented by simple furniture, matting and even, in
our picture (see Ill. 53), by the client's wife dressed in a suitably
restrained smock! The other house, the Aitken Cottage in Cashio
Lane, uses a similar palette of materials in a more formally organised
plan (see Ills. 54 and 55).

The central essay[8] in *The Craftsman* series is devoted to a description
of the house which Barry Parker believed '. . . exemplifies, more than
any other I can call to mind, the application of those qualities and
principles of architecture and furnishing for which I have been
contending'. This is 'Whirriestone' at Rochdale in Lancashire, built

8 'Whirriestone': first design, interior of the living room

for Mrs Ashworth, who was also the client for the unexecuted cottage design mentioned earlier. Parker himself gives a very full description of the house as it was built, but there are facts about the design – giving us an insight into his way of working – which he fails to mention. Fortunately, a large number of original drawings of this house have survived,[9] so it is possible to piece together the story of its development.

The house was designed and built between 1907 and 1909. The site is quite large with the access road along its northern boundary and a slight slope to the south. The house was conceived as a simple rectangular block capped by a steeply pitched hipped roof springing from the first floor cill level. The entrance is from the north and the main living areas face south looking over the gently terraced garden.

All of this can be said of the first design for which a comprehensive set of drawings survive. The exterior shows how well Voysey's vocabulary of materials and forms had been assimilated by Parker. The walls are rough cast and have Voyseyan buttresses at the angles. The windows are organised into ashlar-dressed strips with leaded casements, and two tall chimneys are used to give vertical emphasis to the composition. For some reason, however, this design was then subjected to a series of modifications which almost ruthlessly removed all of the whimsical details of the first design. In their place a strong geometrical discipline was imposed upon both the plans and the elevations. The bay windows were given the same dimensions as the central area of the ingle-nook, and that in the living room was brought directly into line with the ingle. The windows were even more strictly organised into horizontal bands with greater standardisation of dimensions. There is almost an air of modular co-ordination about the design (see Ills. 63–9).

During the construction of the house Mrs Ashworth, who was presumably a widow, remarried and became Mrs Whiteley.[10] Mr Whiteley's arrival led to changes in the requirements. He was evidently a motorist and a billiards player, because designs were prepared for a motor house and a billiard room. An interesting early design for which drawings survive combined these in a two-storey block, with the billiard room on the upper floor. The final solution, however, separated them into two blocks which were placed in an almost Palladian manner on either side of the main house. The roof on the north side was extended forward to form a covered way to shelter motorists and billiards players on their way to and from the house. The whole is completely convincing and Parker's own assessment of it is fully justified. The south façade is wholly symmetrical, with its pair of bay windows and the central position of the long dormer window in the roof. But the asymmetrical location of the double doors on the verandah hints at surprises to be found within. At the north, the game is even more subtle. The central dormer is repeated and the careful placement of the motor house and the billiard room as flanking pavilions stresses the symmetry of the whole. Against this the asymmetry of the entrance, reinforced by the irregular spacing of the columns which carry the covered way, produces a tension which is resolved only upon entering the house.

The interior reaches beyond anything Parker and Unwin had previously achieved in its spatial complexity, whilst being conceived in most respects in accordance with the principles which served them in all of their work. The living room has a major central rectangle, delineated by a continuous frieze and picture rail. This is elaborated both horizontally into the bay and ingle and vertically into a double-height volume overlooked by a landing and a gallery, through which light is brought into the centre of the deep cross-section from continuous dormer windows facing both north and south. As in the idealised design from *The Art of Building a Home* this space can accommodate a full range of domestic activity and extends further through an ingenious and beautifully detailed folding screen into a study. When this is opened the whole volume of the house is perceived. The effect of this is an elaborate spatial counterpoint in which the eye constantly reads different volumetric combinations. In some views the relationship between the ingle-nook and the bay window dominates, in others the vertical flow through the double-height space takes over, but it is all held together by the strong horizontals of the frieze which ensures that one is never unnerved by the complexity and that the house remains a setting for domestic life, fulfilling the aim which Parker and Unwin set down in *The Art of Building a Home* to create '... rooms which can form backgrounds, fitting and dignified, at the time and in our memories, for all those little scenes, those acts of kindness and small duties, as well as the scenes of deep emotion and trial, which make up the drama of our lives at home.'[11]

The relationship between the stair and the ingle-nook is as well contrived as ever, allowing storage cupboards and shelves to fall naturally into place. A rendered perspective survives showing heraldic decoration on the walls of the double-height space (see Ill. 66). Fortunately this was never executed, perhaps it was a draughtsman's flight of fancy, and the interior avoids any of the stylistic naivety of the early designs. The joinery detailing and all of the purpose-made furniture have a refinement which looks forward to the later more abstract conceptions of architecture of the twentieth century, rather than backwards to nostalgic revivalism.

The house is the summation of all that Parker and Unwin had been working towards in their earlier houses. It achieves its ends by the use of simple constructional methods and by playing-off the complexity of its interior against the simplicity, even serenity, of its exterior. Its basis in the Arts and Crafts tradition is evident in its whole conception, from the materials used, and the manner in which they are expressed, to the conventional respect for good orientation. The exterior is closer to Voysey than any other of their houses, but the interior is unlike anything he ever conceived. Voysey's plans are, as a rule, highly compartmentalised. Their quality derives from their decoration and furnishing and their beautifully controlled lighting. Spatial complexity was not an important matter for him, although in and around staircases he was usually quite expansive.

The relation of Parker and Unwin's work to that of Voysey is very important. Gustav Stickley made a comparison between Parker's approach to the design of furniture and that of Voysey.[12]

In Mr. Parker's furniture one is occasionally reminded in line and finish of the Art Nouveau development in France. But it is a subdued Art Nouveau, shorn of pretence and whimsicality; an Art Nouveau humbled and purified. On the other hand, Mr. Voysey's furniture suggests more his inherited appreciation of the good qualities of the old Jacobean furniture.

This is an interesting analysis, particularly in the light of Pevsner's assertion of the influence which Voysey had upon Art Nouveau itself in *Pioneers of Modern Design*.[13] It is interesting to compare Voysey's design for an oak chesterfield for 'The Homestead' at Frinton, dated February 1907, with Parker's contemporary reversible desk chair at 'Whirriestone'. In both there is a clear enjoyment of the essentials of construction and in giving expression to the demands of function,

9 Oak chesterfield by C. F.
A. Voysey, designed for
'The Homestead', Frinton-
on-Sea

10 Reversible chair
designed by Barry Parker
for 'Whirriestone'

which suggest the influence of Voysey on the younger man, but
Parker's design displays a delight in sheer complexity which would
have been impossible for Voysey. In this we have something of the
essential difference between their work at all scales. Peter Davey[14] has
shrewdly described Voysey as 'The Pathfinder' for the Arts and Crafts
movement in architecture. Parker's work bears witness to this, but
also shows, most conspicuously at 'Whirriestone', that the genre was
capable of sustaining fruitful developments which went beyond
anything which Voysey himself attempted.

Gardens and Non-Domestic Buildings

As the architect of the Garden City, Parker inevitably saw the design of a house as inseparable from the layout of its garden. In *The Art of Building a Home* gardens receive virtually no attention, but ten years on, after the experience of New Earswick, Letchworth and Hampstead, and of many individual houses, he had formed quite emphatic opinions on the subject. With the huge amount of house building in England during this period – the inspiration for Muthesius's visit – gardening had become a prime interest amongst the middle classes. Gertrude Jekyll's activities and, particularly the series of books which she wrote, beginning in 1899 and culminating in 1912 with *Gardens for Small Country Houses*,[1] are an indication of the extent of this new-found passion, as is the scope of Baillie Scott's book of 1906.[2]

Parker offers a view of the garden which is totally consistent with his Arts and Crafts beliefs. He is particularly strong in his insistence that most gardens must be contrived and that attempts to imitate nature are wrong. 'A garden should be a work of art and should glory in it. As soon as it attempts to appear artless it oversteps the bounds of art.'

On a more practical front he shows a keen appreciation of the English climate in his enthusiasm for 'garden rooms, loggias, stoeps [a concession to his American readers], balconies, verandahs, summer houses, porches, etc.'. He says that these are more likely to be used if they are a part of the house, rather than separate structures, and insists that such amenities are important even in a small house. He even puts in a word for the humble window box!

In the city proper, Parker sees that 'courts, quadrangles and closes' can offer a viable alternative to traditional terraced arrangements of small houses. In a series of essays on site planning he takes up once more the theme of quadrangle housing which Unwin had discussed in *The Art of Building a Home* and produces a detailed version of the chequerboard site plan which had been presented in the project for 'Cottages near a town' in 1901.[3] A fragment of this design was built in the pair of cottages at Starbeck near Harrogate, but its full validity only becomes apparent in a large-scale development.

It is in these essays that Parker most closely approaches Unwin's work in *Town Planning in Practice*. There is, for all their shared values

11 'An irregular town', from Raymond Unwin's *Town Planning in Practice*; drawing by Charles Wade

and ideals, however, a fundamental difference in approach. Unwin bases his proposals upon his analysis of the necessary qualities of the urban scene and particularly acknowledges the influence of Camillo Sitte and Stübben.[4] Parker begins from an analysis of functional concerns in the design of small houses, such as how they may be placed on the ground to satisfy requirements for good orientation of both house and garden, and for privacy. The results are less picturesque than those suggested by Unwin's illustrations – particularly as they were presented in Charles Wade's beautiful drawings – but contain many interesting possibilities which might have beneficially influenced English housing design if Parker's plans for publication had come to fruition. Housing practice in England had to wait until the 1960s and Leslie Martin and Lionel March's studies of 'Land Use and Built Forms'[5] for a revival of this kind of interest in the geometry of housing.

In the years before the publication of *The Craftsman* essays, Parker and Unwin's practice, in common with those of most Arts and Crafts architects, built few public buildings. The Garden City did, however, provide the opportunity to take a look at the design of industrial buildings from a new standpoint. It was undesirable simply to reproduce the stereotypes of the nineteenth-century industrial towns in this new setting and a number of important experiments were produced. The most elaborate of these was the large factory for the Spirella Company of Great Britain.[6] Its architect was Cecil Hignett, who had worked for Parker and Unwin for many years following his apprenticeship with Edgar Wood in Manchester. Hignett became something of a specialist in industrial buildings and it is likely that he had a hand in the design of the St Edmundsbury Weaving Works (see Ills. 92 and 93) which Parker described in *The Craftsman*. The concern with lighting expressed in the description was to be a major factor in the much larger Spirella building.

Within Parker and Unwin's social, even 'socialist', vision the meeting room had a special place. The description of the Guest House in William Morris's *News from Nowhere* was a potent image with which they would certainly have been familiar and was closely paralleled in a number of designs for clubs and public halls.

. . . we were presently within doors, and standing in a hall with a floor of marble mosaic and an open timber roof . . . everything about the place was handsome and generously solid as to material; and though it was not very large, one felt in it that exhilarating sense of space and freedom which satisfactory architecture always gives to an unanxious man who is in the habit of using his eyes.[7]

This is a difficult programme for any architect to live up to but something of Parker and Unwin's acceptance of the challenge can be found in the project for a Working Girls' Club in Manchester (see Ill. 95). This is a curious, but not unsuccessful, combination of their familiar vernacular manner and elements which clearly derive from Josef Hoffmann's Palais Stoclet in Brussels of 1905.

The Craftsman series came to a close with two essays on the restoration of existing buildings. These are conceived very much in the spirit of Morris's declaration in the Manifesto of the Society for the Protection of Ancient Buildings, but adapted to the more pragmatic needs of a busy practising architect who, whilst remaining a man of principle, is reluctant to turn down an interesting job. His work at King's Langley Priory is a clear illustration of how Parker's practice was informed by his theoretical position:

. . . we should alter old work as little as possible, whenever practicable making necessary modifications in the form of definite *additions*, and never replacing old work with new except where this is constructionally necessary, or where it is requisite to fulfil the purpose of the building . . .

Postscript

Within two years of the publication of the last of these essays in *The Craftsman* Parker and Unwin's partnership came to an end, after eighteen years in which they had played a central role in giving form and reality to Ebenezer Howard's vision of the Garden City and had conducted an architectural practice which evolved a unique and valuable interpretation of the Arts and Crafts view of the English house.

Unwin moved into public service and, through a number of influential appointments, was able to carry his experience over in forming the basis for British housing practice after the First World War.[1] Following his retirement in 1930 he continued to work energetically for the cause of town planning, both at home and overseas. He was President of the Royal Institute of British Architects between 1931 and 1933 and was knighted in 1932. In 1937 he received the Royal Gold Medal for Architecture. Throughout the 1920s and 1930s Unwin was a frequent visitor to the United States and in 1936 was elected Visiting Professor at Columbia University, a post which he held until his death (at his daughter's home at Old Lyme, Connecticut) on 28 June 1940.

After Unwin's departure Parker continued to work from the office in Letchworth. There was much work to be done in the Garden City and, after the war, his extensive experience in housing allowed him to find almost tailor-made commissions within the government-funded housing programme in which Unwin played such a prominent role. This work reached its climax in 1927 when he was appointed by the City of Manchester to advise on the planning of the huge garden suburb of Wythenshawe for a projected population of 100,000. Two other important commissions came from overseas. First, in 1915, he produced an ambitious proposal for remodelling the central area of Oporto in Portugal. This was exhibited at the Royal Academy in 1916 but was never executed. In 1917 he travelled to Brazil where he spent two years as consultant to the city of Sao Paulo in the design of a garden suburb. This was completed and Parker's photograph albums, which are preserved at Letchworth, contain a number of photographs of it under construction. In 1942 he retired from practice and died in Letchworth in 1947.

After 1914 the manner of building houses to which Parker and Unwin were wholeheartedly committed fell completely from favour. Voysey, by then in late middle-age, built nothing more of significance, although he lived until 1941. Mackintosh's practice was, to all intents, finished by 1910 when the second phase of the Glasgow School of Art was completed. Lutyens, who was never devoted to the theories and dogmas of the Arts and Crafts, had begun to use classical elements in his houses as early as 1901, and gave the 'high game of Palladio' full expression for the first time in Heathcote at Ilkley, completed in 1906. Baillie Scott also made the transition to the new style although not, apparently, without deep misgivings.

There is a particular charm about this eighteenth-century manner of building. It has a certain sedate primness. It has a well-behaved and well-drilled aspect, and being somewhat artificial and conventional finds itself more at home in town or suburb than in the country. It does not suffer so much from mechanical workmanship as the older manner of building, and since it imposes some restraint on natural gesture it may be compared to a strait-waistcoat which may be wisely worn by those who have lost the power of natural and graceful movement.[2]

Although Barry Parker and Raymond Unwin were no longer designing individual houses of the style and quality of their major designs of 1896 to 1914, they were able in their respective private and official capacities to continue to pursue their deep commitment to the improvement of housing for all sorts of men to the ends of their lives. The twists and turns of taste and fashion may have meant that their particular way of building fell from favour at the time of the First World War, but through legislation and practice they were able to bring to fruition the dreams which they had in those early days in Derbyshire when they sat together 'evening after evening' working on designs for the miners' church at Barrow Hill.

In a broad, social sense their legacy lies in the contribution which they made in satisfying the Englishman's expectation, unique in Europe, of living in a house with a private garden – even if it is in a suburb. As designers their achievement may be measured in the quality of the buildings and towns which they created. As I have tried to show, the success and special qualities of these owed much to their devotion to the application of principle in design. Parker's essays in *The Craftsman* are a clear statement of the nature of his functional and idealistic goals, and analysis of the houses he used to illustrate these reveals the importance of geometrical order in his work. Perhaps most of all, however, we should rely on the evidence of our eyes in arriving at an assessment of these houses. Overriding all else is their pervading sense of providing a deeply sympathetic setting for the vision of domestic life which lies deep in the hearts of most Englishmen.

Part Two

◇◇

Modern Country Homes in England,
BARRY PARKER

1

◆◇◆

Introduction

In nineteen hundred and one a book entitled 'The Art of Building a Home' was published. Looking back to the publication of this book, and finding that attempts to put into practice the principles there laid down have strengthened and deepened my conviction as to their truth, I gladly respond to the suggestion that I should show how far we have been able to carry out these principles in our work, and what has been the result of the attempt to do this. What follows will naturally fall into sequel form, and therefore must be prefaced by a summary, as brief as possible, of the main principles laid down in 'The Art of Building a Home'. I now feel that the book might well be summed up as a plea for honesty, and realise too that it arose from a conviction that a different spirit was necessary from that which prevailed in the practice of domestic architecture before it could again become a living art, and also from an earnest desire to discover that spirit.

We saw there could be only one true way of going to work, and that was to build in the simplest and most direct way possible just that which would best fulfil the functions and meet the requirements in each instance, trusting solely to direct and straightforward construction, frankly acknowledged and shown, to produce beauty, instead of to decoration and ornament, pilasters, cornices, entablatures, pediments and what not, superimposed or added and hiding or disguising the constructional features. The tendency to disregard the decorative qualities inherent in the material used in construction, or resulting from the processes of construction, the desire to cover all these up, and not only fail to make the most of them but to neglect them, and to put in their place 'features' supposed to be ornamental but known not to be useful, we felt was wrong.

We noticed that those about to build their own homes seldom seemed to consider what were their actual and real needs and requirements, or what would best enable them to live the fullest and completest lives they were capable of, or what would best express their own personalities, individualities and aims. They considered anything but these. They would perhaps think what impression their proposed home would make upon callers, what their neighbours, friends and relatives had, or would expect them to have; what was

37

customary in the rank of life to which they belonged; what they had been accustomed to, and what they could afford: but seldom what would best fit them and their real needs. We conceived it to be the architect's business to use any influence he might have with his clients to induce them to consider these real needs and weaken their adherence to mere conventions; to point out to them that the mere fact that they were able to afford what other people had was not sufficient reason for having it, without thought as to whether it would add to or hinder their fullest lives.

The architect should create for each client not merely what is accepted conventionally as a satisfactory house. He should aim at doing far more than this: at creating a true setting for true lives, stamped with the personalities, individualities, characters and influence of those lives. He must not encourage the tendency to let the household make too great a sacrifice for the sake of callers, and he must not evince as little tendency to get down to fundamentals as his clients so often do.

To enable him to accomplish this at all fully we felt it was necessary that his influence should be extended down to the smallest details of decoration and furnishing; for it was essential that he should be in a position to conceive each house as a whole, as completely as any other work of art might be, and to have it carried out in its entirety. This was impossible if others were called in to decorate and furnish, for they would inevitably fail to complete his scheme.

Just as in the building itself our hope lay in revealing the beauties inherent in construction and the materials used in construction, so hope lay in making the useful and necessary things in the house beautiful, instead of disregarding them, or covering them up with what we supposed to be beautiful.

We felt very strongly that as soon as anything useful or decorative ceased to take just that form which was 'most constructional' and took a form constructionally less sound (because supposed to be more beautiful), it was outside the limits of a true work of art.

We knew that the choice of the right materials out of which to build must come first, and that these would almost certainly prove to be the materials most readily to hand; that one lesson to be learned from the work of past ages was the probability that the building materials to be found in a locality were artistically and practically the best to use in that locality, that they would harmonise best with their surroundings, and that to conceive forms suited to them was most likely to result in that completeness of a perfect whole at which we should aim.

In short, we conceived it to be within the architect's sphere to provide a home fitted to and expressing the life to be lived within it, complete down to the last detail. So he must ever strive to deepen his insight, and gain a wider, a freer, less prejudiced and franker outlook upon his work.

It is all a question of attitude of mind. We are so timid. Of this we have signs on every hand. The first railway carriages (naturally perhaps) took the forms of stage coaches put upon rails, and only gradually are railway carriages evolving into forms suited to their conditions. Our first motor cars were carriages without horses, with the engines awkwardly fitted into a form of vehicle contrived to suit other means of locomotion, and we are only gradually evolving forms suited to the new means. The attitude of mind which conduces to success in designing a motor is that of one who, clearly grasping what will lead to the greatest efficiency in the engines and to the comfort and convenience of the travellers, conceives the form best adapted to secure these: not the attitude of mind of one who, following tradition, accepts the forms it has arrived at for horse-drawn vehicles, and understands the problem as one of applying motor engines to these vehicles.

Why should we take it for granted that anything new must imitate what it supersedes? Linoleums as much like carpets as possible, and American leather to imitate real leather. The first iron bedsteads were fashioned and painted and grained to simulate wooden ones. Concrete building blocks have not yet been long enough in use for them to have passed out of the stage in which it is taken for granted they must be made to imitate either stones or bricks. Neither have steel-framed buildings been with us long enough for us to have the temerity to give them a form which frankly acknowledges them as such. The same is true of ferro-concrete structures. We still feel we must try and give them the appearance of being either stone or brick built.

I have taken most of my illustrations of the application of abstract principles from outside what has been the sphere of my own work, because I thought I might by doing so make the principles stand out more clearly, and so simplify the application of them to the designing of all that goes to make up the externals of a home.

In some respects considerable progress has of course been made during the past ten years. We no longer, even at the worst, have our physical and artistic susceptibilities bruised by polished fire irons, which no one ever dreams of using, laid in a fender as a trap for us. Many door fastenings now are not buried in a hole dug in the wood of the door, and some are guiltless of any case or covering, and are as pleasant in form as were many of the beautiful old latches.

In every house there should be one room which takes the place of what in olden times was known as 'the houseplace' or 'hall' as the centre of the common life of the household. Although we sometimes still find such a room in small houses, larger houses have come to be divided into a number of rooms, such as dining rooms, drawing rooms, libraries, morning rooms, and what not, none of which forms a real centre for the life of the household.

In the house here illustrated, 'The Homestead', I have tried to

12 'The Homestead',
Chesterfield: plan

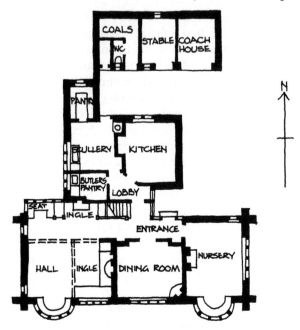

reinstate 'the houseplace'. There is a comparatively small dining room, and the rest of that space which would have usually been broken up into a number of other rooms is devoted to one large 'houseplace'. The result is that instead of the household always being in one or other of several comparatively small and uninteresting rooms while the rest stand unoccupied, they live in spaciousness which gives breadth and dignity.

'The Homestead' stands a few miles out of Chesterfield, in Derbyshire; and being in a district where stone is plentiful it was built of a gritstone quarried in the neighbourhood. This stone has also been used in forming the fireplaces and ingles, and is left both as the exterior and interior finish of all windows.

The house was placed well back from the high road which runs past the south front; but in order not to sacrifice any of this precious south front and view to entrances, and to secure it all for the windows of the principal rooms, the drive was taken round to the north side, and the front door placed in that side, but at a point where it is abundantly sheltered and protected.

Entering this house, then, we come at once into a limb of 'The Great Hall'. An essential of such a hall is that no traffic should pass through or across it, or its comfort would be gone; but as the staircase must be in it, and the entrance and many other doors must open into it, all coming and going must be contrived in a part devoted exclusively to these purposes.

Part of the hall is carried to the full height of two storeys of the rest of the house. Across one end runs the minstrel gallery securing the

13 'The Homestead' from the south

14 'The Homestead': the hall or 'houseplace'. The large ingle-nook is to the right. The small ingle and window seat are beneath the gallery at the rear of the room.

charm of music coming from a hidden source. The floor is of oak blocks laid on concrete, which produces a silent footfall.

The photographs will show how the structure of both building and furniture provides the decoration of this room. The stonework of the walls of the ingles, of the windows and fireplaces, and the timber in the wood-framed partition, which forms one wall of the bedroom over the low-ceiled part of the great hall, are all left uncovered.

In this framed partition is a little window looking down from the bedroom into the hall. Even the smoke flue above the main fireplace stands out in carved stonework from the wall.

In the west wall of the hall is an arch built up for the time being, but arranged to open into a billiard room to be built on at this end of the house. The central part of the fitment on the wall of the hall is so designed that it can be removed to a position designed for it in the billiard room when this room is built.

I was permitted to design all the furniture throughout the house, together with the carpets, the metal work on doors and cupboards, the gas fittings and decoration. The latter is entirely the work of artists' hands, and consists of stone and wood carving, embroidery and metal work. Most of the metal work is in what is known as silveroid, which does not tarnish and is silver-like in colour.

Where the walls in this house are plastered they are left rough from the wood float, a little colouring matter being mixed with the plaster.

The stonework has been allowed to give the keynote to the interior colour scheme, which is the same throughout the house. The plaster is cream coloured, and forms a pleasant contrast to the peacock blues of the carpets, curtains and upholsteries.

A house constructed, furnished and decorated as this has been entails practically no expense in redecoration and painting – the ironwork, of which there is little, and the doors being the only things that require painting outside, and the interior walls, stonework and woodwork need only occasional cleaning; nothing requires renewal. This obviously effects a great annual saving.

The ease with which such a house can be kept clean, and the fact that dusting is reduced to the minimum, may not be noticed by the reader unless pointed out. This is partly the result of using fixed furniture, and furniture designed for its place, partly of leaving construction as decoration, and partly because the scheme having been conceived as a whole is therefore complete, and the temptation to be constantly adding to it is removed.

Above all the warnings I would give to the designer of small houses would come one against the conscious effort to gain picturesqueness. Let the exterior be always the logical outcome and expression of well thought out interior arrangements. I would on the other hand call his attention to the fact that perhaps the most potent factors in artistic success or failure in designing small houses is in the relation of solids to voids, of window spaces to wall spaces, and in the proportions and distribution of these.

Every turn of the road reminds us that we seldom find satisfactory solutions of the difficulties that the modern demand for lighter rooms has created, and how frequently this demand upsets the charming relations of window spaces to wall spaces which make much of the old work so lovely.

2

◇◆◇

Solving an Architectural Problem

When called upon to design a house, the first thing a designer has to do is to get a real knowledge of his client. It is almost as difficult for an architect to design a house really successfully for perfect strangers, as it is for a portrait painter to paint a stranger successfully.

With as complete a knowledge as he can get of the people for whose lives he is to create a home, and of their requirements and tastes, the designer must go on to the site and let it dictate to him what shall be the interior arrangement of the house, and largely what shall be its exterior treatment. The site must suggest the interior arrangement because the contours and falls of the land must have their influence on the design, or the house can never be one which will look as if it had come there naturally, a pleasant part of its surroundings, and not a 'foreign body'.

Considerations of true economy also lead to careful study of the falls and contours of the land. The position of the approach, and the point to which the drains must be brought of course determine much; but perhaps the site dictates most through consideration of the aspects of the various rooms and the outlook from their windows.

We no longer regard a house, as did our ancestors, as being primarily a shelter for those who lived chiefly out of doors. We now look upon it as a home in which to spend most of our time. This has effected not only a change in the nature of the sites we choose, but very greatly also our views as to planning. A sheltered situation was considered the first essential in the old days; now many would sacrifice this to gain good prospects from the windows. The site should also be allowed to suggest the exterior treatment to be adopted, or that feeling of fitting in with its surroundings which I have attempted to describe will not be gained.

Perhaps the use of local materials may not be quite so emphatically suggested for a country site as it is for a town site, because in some cases it is conceivable that a material brought from a distance might be found which would fit in with the surroundings, and take its place in the landscape almost as well as one found in the district; but we learn from the past that in those towns in which the greatest consistency in the use of certain building materials has been maintained, the greatest sense of unity and completeness has resulted. This has not been brought about by deliberate regard for a sense of the fitness of these materials, but by the fact that, being the local materials, they were the cheapest and most available. Now that building materials brought from a distance can compete in price with those in the locality, and so this practical consideration is removed, it behoves the architect to be more alive to the importance of using local materials from his sense of fitness, and his desire to regard his work as taking its place in a complete picture.

Sometimes on the site an almost complete conception of what his building should be presents itself to the mind of the architect, and then he is extremely fortunate, and the result of his efforts is likely to be more happy than at any other time.

The best buildings always appear to have been almost a complete conception. Their plans and elevations seem inseparable, the former account for the latter from the bottom to the top. The degree to which this can be obtained depends upon the grasp and mastery of the designer.

When a conception of a building as a whole does not present itself, it is most satisfactory to start from the plans entirely, making them first thoroughly useful and fit, then, being satisfied with these, to go on to the elevations, letting them grow, letting them suggest and almost make themselves.

This will pave the way for modifications in the plans, as the elevations may require, for their improvement in balance, grouping and construction; always, of course, being on guard against endangering the utility of the plans.

As I have said before, let the exterior be the logical outcome and expression of well thought out interior arrangements. Very much depends on a proper understanding of the right relationship between plans and elevations. It is not uncommon for plans to be made to fit in with a conception of what the designer wishes the elevations to be, and this is radically wrong. Sometimes plans, if not actually worked through elevations, are certainly influenced by possible exterior effect more than is justifiable; first secure logical plans, which it can be seen will result in satisfactory grouping and 'pile up', and from these evolve elevations. And here let me guard against the misunderstanding that I am advocating anything so absurd as the method, adopted I believe by some designers, of planning the various floors of a building and then considering how that building is to be roofed; the veriest novice at the work must of necessity be thinking as much of his roof plan when making his ground floor plan as he is of the ground floor plan itself. I am only suggesting that the man who goes first for suitable logical plans, including his roof plan, and next for elevations which come naturally from and express these, is on the right line for success. So we see how inevitably anyone must be going the wrong way to work who takes a design made to fit one set of conditions, and considers what adaptations and modifications will

15 House at Minehead:
ground floor plan

make it fit another. We must not suppose a design used for any other site or adapted to any other conditions than those for which it was made can ever result in anything but failure.

For the house used here to illustrate the foregoing principles the site at Minehead in Somerset is of very great beauty but presenting exceptional difficulties. If an architect does not secure for the principal living room in a British country house of this size all the sunshine there may be at any time of the day, on any day of the year, he cannot be said to have been entirely successful. Now from the site in question there was a view to the north which it was imperative should be seen from the living room, but the finest view was out eastward. So it was necessary to have windows also on that side, as well as those for sunshine on the south, and in addition a peep down the valley westward could not be missed. To secure all these for the one room was a problem, but it was not enough merely to do this.

Every room, no matter how many windows it may have, seems to have a certain trend or 'direction' of its own. It turns its face one way, and much depends upon seeing that it turns its face aright, that it has the right 'direction' given to it. It is very easy to find a room which, though it has windows looking where the room should look, still does anything but face that way. It is even very easy to find a room with windows commanding a fine view through which that view will seldom be enjoyed because the 'direction' of its plan is wrong. So here at Minehead it was necessary that the room should turn its face eastward, and this could only be secured by arranging that from the parts of the room in which those using it would naturally stand or sit when pursuing their customary occupations, they would command the view out east.

Therefore the fireplace must be in the west wall, for all through the winter months the life in such a house centres round the living-room fire. And it must be seen to that the big east window shall be in that part of the room in which the household will congregate during the summer months, that is, in the part furthest removed from the traffic routes, and from the doors and draughts. So every effort had to be made to give the living room an easterly 'direction'. The peep down the valley westward was secured from the west window in the living room across the open courtyard, and down the vista of the pergola. It was desirable that most of the bedrooms and also the dining room should enjoy a southern exposure, while the latter, like the living room, had an eastern 'direction' given it, and gained the fine eastern view. Stables which could be reached under shelter were necessary, and how to place them without cutting off any sunshine, or destroying views from the house was part of the problem. Further, the approach was from the north, and the land fell rapidly from the south to the north.

All the walls were built of stone quarried a few yards from the site. On the outside they were rough-cast with local lime and gravel which gave them a beautiful cream colour. On the inside, they were finished with Cheddar lime worked up to a rough stucco surface, and left in the clear white which resulted, without any applied decoration or colour. The roof timbers and wall framing were allowed to decorate the living room, and the roof was laid by local workmen with straw thatch in accordance with local traditional methods. On the first floor is a gallery looking down into the living room.

3

◇◈◇

Building for Light

Some little repetition here of subject matter which appeared in 'The Art of Building a Home' seems inevitable. It was there pointed out that an appreciation of the importance of the right relation to one another of the doors, windows and fireplaces must exist in the mind of anyone who is to succeed in designing a comfortable living room; that in a rectangular room which has one door, one window and one fireplace the most comfortable distribution of these is that shown in diagram one [Ill. 16], but that in a room which has more than one window the pleasantest is that shown in diagram two [Ill. 16]. These two diagrams must only be taken as showing general principles capable of application in an infinite variety of ways to endless different forms of rooms, and of course they do not apply to bedrooms, for in a bedroom the bed should occupy just the position the fireplace should occupy in a living room. Rooms planned on the lines indicated in these diagrams are comfortable not only because those who sit round the fires in them are out of the draughts and well in the light, but because they may be free from the apprehension of disturbance caused by other members of the household entering or leaving, and are where they see the room and command the outlook from it to the best advantage.

But we must realise that it is not enough to secure actual comfort; the planner must also give the feeling and appearance of comfort. Some rooms have a welcoming, cheery, hospitable aspect which adds something every day to the sum of happiness of their fortunate users; others, which give as great actual physical comfort perhaps, are quite devoid of this charm, and we cannot easily overestimate the importance of constant study to gain it.

One can find excuses for most things, but there are faults in house planning which seem inexcusable, and among these might we not include a living room planned with the fireplace where the room is darkest, or with a door opening right across the fire, and a kitchen planned in such a way that the cook will when cooking block out the light that would (were she not there) fall upon the range, or having doors on each side of the range as shown in diagram three [Ill. 16]?

There is a common supposition that all small rooms are necessarily most economical of space when square in form. For a small bedroom

47

16 Room arrangement
diagrams

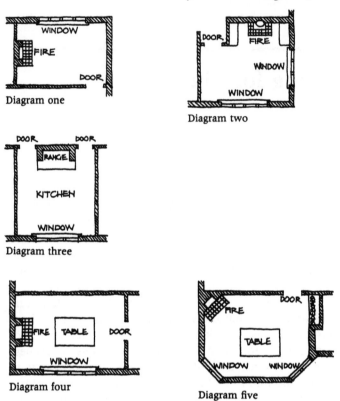

Diagram one

Diagram two

Diagram three

Diagram four

Diagram five

the square form is not the most economical because all the space the bed does not occupy comes to be merely a narrow passageway around it. A room oblong in plan works out better, for there space is left at the foot of the bed available for dressing in. Neither is the form of room shown in diagram four [Ill. 16] really necessarily the best for a small dining room, though it is generally taken as a matter of course to be so. Something on the lines indicated in the other plan has many advantages over it. No one sits at the dining table with his back to the fire roasting himself and keeping the heat from the others. No one sits in his own light or where he keeps the light from falling on the table, and the door does not open right behind one of those at the table, but where there is a little space between them.

The illustrations which follow now are of a house designed for a site at Northwood near Stoke-on-Trent. The section through the house shows how the internal court was planned to have the roof sloping down to it on all sides to make sure that light should always flood it, and that it should bring brightness and cheeriness and airiness right into the midst of the house. We have all seen small courts the effect of which was the very reverse of this, even perhaps of well-like darkness, and so we realise the importance of avoiding this pitfall. The pleasantness of this court is enhanced when the framing

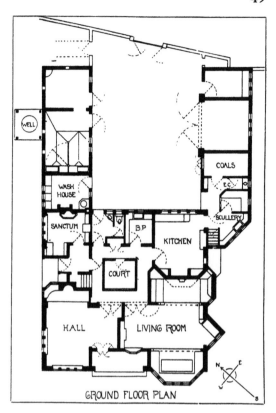

17 House at Northwood,
near Stoke-on-Trent:
ground floor plan and
cross-section

GROUND FLOOR PLAN

separating court from corridor is made open framing by sliding down the glazed sashes which fill it. The corridors running around this court are then converted into open cloisters, and in so sheltered a position they can be left open for all but the very coldest weather. On to these cloisters the rooms open with wide double doors, so that it is possible, even though the house occupies an exposed site on a hill, to have the rooms open to the fresh air to an unusual extent. The sun, if it does shine, shines into the living room from morning to night. The dining table is placed in a windowed dining recess from which a full view of the fire is gained.

Not long ago, I visited again the first house I ever designed [Moorlands, Buxton, Derbyshire, built for his parents in 1895]. In many respects it shows immature work, of course, but the fireplace had some of the advantages of the ingle fireplaces of olden times. The light of the fire filled the whole recess, making it contrast pleasantly and invitingly with the rest of the room. The ingle made it possible to have the grate standing and the fire burning right out in the room, protected from cross draughts. This resulted in a great proportion of the heat which in an ordinary fireplace goes up the chimney coming into the room, and gave three sides of the fire on which there could be seats instead of only one. The more completely a fire-grate is recessed

18 House at Northwood: living room interior showing the ingle-nook and 'proscenium arch' of the bay containing the piano

19 House at Northwood: the hall ingle with a view into the internal courtyard

into a wall the more heat goes up the chimney and the fewer are the points of view from which the fire can be seen. If an ingle is to be a success one essential is that a full view of the fire be obtained from all seats within the ingle. Work done with the object of gaining certain definite advantages of utility or beauty, which one really values and appreciates, work which simply, honestly and straightforwardly done, generally comes out right. At Northwood it will be noticed that

20 House at Northwood: view from the courtyard into the 'sanctum'. The courtyard has ingeniously detailed sliding sash windows which allow it to be fully enclosed or open at will.

21 House at Northwood: the entrance porch displays Parker's characteristic enjoyment of creating a play between free composition and symmetry

22 Sketch for the hall at
'Moorlands', Buxton

the hall ingle is contrived under the staircase and landing, the flue
being brought over in stonework on to the arch. The porch is also
arranged under the landing.

Our client possessed some beautiful Oriental pottery and a few
good Japanese wood-block prints; these were used, the former in
glazed cupboards in the living room ingle, and the latter on various
parts of the wall surfaces. With this exception I was privileged to
design everything in the house and to plan the garden.

4

◇◆◇

A Study of Personality in Building

The way in which a man may stamp his own personality upon his house by having it, and everything in it, designed for him by one in close touch with him, while at the same time giving the architect an opportunity to create a unity of effect, is perhaps more strongly exemplified by the accompanying plans and photographs than by any which have preceded them. The owner of the house illustrated could not have so stamped his personality upon a house, such as he might have found ready to hand, nor could the furniture so obviously have expressed his tastes and character had he collected it from various sources. By a life spent in close study of the characters and customs of many nations, perhaps more especially of the Japanese, he has gained that breadth of outlook which much travel alone can give, and has come to feel that we have much to learn from the older civilisations of the East, civilisations which, on the other hand, we of the West are beginning to mar.

So when he came to settle in England it was his wish to do this in a home and among surroundings which would make it possible for him to practise and demonstrate to others what he had come to believe in. His position being as follows: that it is everyone's first duty to society and to himself or herself to be always in the most perfect health possible. He even goes so far as to say that few of us are justified in being ill, claiming that only when in perfect health are we capable of our best in any sphere, and that it is our duty never to give anything short of our best.

A wide outlook from his windows was essential to his attitude of mind, so the site chosen was on one of the highest hills of the Surrey Downs – the summit of the 'White Hill' at Caterham, commanding some of the widest and most beautiful views in England. Believing in the physical and perhaps even greater mental alertness and agility resulting from the practice of the Japanese art of self-defence, jiu-jitsu, one of the principal rooms of his house had to be so planned as to give ample facilities for the practice of this art, while at the same time it was not to be spoiled for the many other uses to which it might be put. On the accompanying plans this room is called the gymnasium.

It was not possible to secure quite as much sunshine in this room as

53

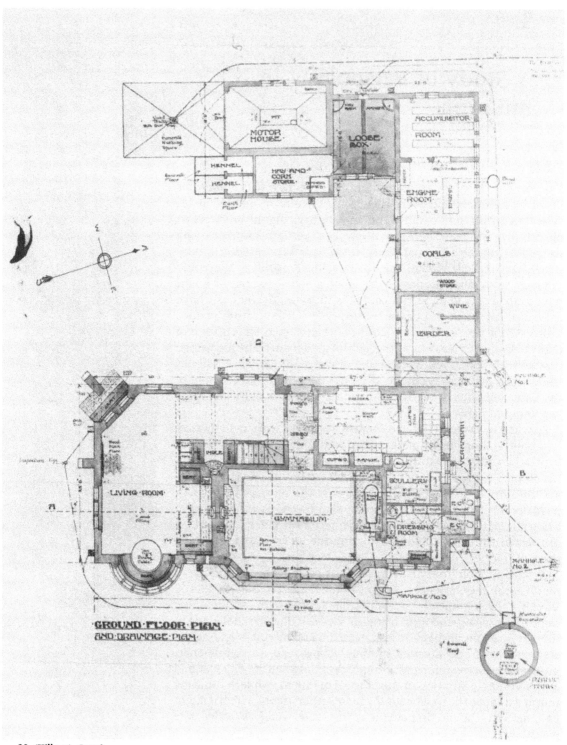

23 'Hilltop', Caterham:
ground floor plan from
original ½ inch scale
working drawing

24 'Hilltop': the small ingle-nook in the passage leading to the living room

25 'Hilltop': the gymnasium with the client, Mr Steers, practising his jiu-jitsu. The mural decoration is by Hugh Wallis.

could have been wished, partly owing to considerations for its privacy and partly to the necessary position for the living room. The gymnasium, however, gets all the northeast, east and southeast sun there may be, the morning sun that is, and its use as a gymnasium is almost entirely in the morning. The front of this room being composed of rolling shutters and large, opening windows through which one enters on to an exercising lawn, terminating in an open-air swimming bath, necessitated extreme privacy and therefore an aspect away from the road which runs by the south end of the house. The room is carried to the full height of the house – two storeys – so, when the rolling shutters, together with the French windows on either side of them and the row of windows above are all open, as is almost always the case, the room is a very high one with practically one side quite open; in fact, it becomes a three-walled room. This sense of openness and airiness so experienced would be unobtainable in a less lofty room, even though equally open in front. The floor, like a dancing floor, is carried on springs, and is covered with Japanese reed mats two inches thick. A dressing room and bath are connected with the gymnasium.

In summer, with mattresses thrown down at night upon the reed mats and the front thrown open, this room becomes one of the most delightful sleeping apartments imaginable. The Japanese custom of having no rooms set aside exclusively for sleeping in is one that the owner holds we might well adopt. We are coming to see the great advantage of substituting fewer and larger rooms for the many small ones custom has until quite recently made us think necessary to our comfort. Do we perhaps make a mistake, those of us living in small houses, in not making more use for our day-time occupations of the space set aside for bedrooms? Certainly, we have to guard against the tendency to provide a room for each purpose for which one may conceivably be required. We see how over and over again lives have been made so complicated by the provision of facilities for every possible occupation that to do any one thing thoroughly becomes impossible.

The decoration of the gymnasium was undertaken by Mr Hugh Wallis of Altrincham. He was asked to go to Caterham, to stand in the middle of the room and imagine he was standing in a green glade or clearing in a forest, then to paint on the rough plaster of the walls the vistas among the trees, their foliage, boles, stems and branches, glimpses of sky and distant landscape, and in the foreground, flowers in the grass. When the artist reached Caterham, the spirit of the delightful Surrey scenery surrounding him took so great a hold of his imagination that he had perforce to reproduce it in his delightfully decorative style. The vistas between the trees widened out and became filled with glimpses of distant country, broadening finally into wide peaceful scenes in the luxuriant Surrey countryside.

To proceed with the account of why the house was planned just in the way it was. The finest views being to the southeast, south and southwest, these were naturally secured for the chief living room, which at the same time was so placed as to leave unimpaired the beautiful southeast view from the gymnasium. At this end of the living room a semi-circular bay, with seats fitted round it, was built, and the round table at which all meals are taken was placed there.

The chief meals are taken in what is at the times when they are served the sunniest and lightest corner of the house.

Part of this L-shaped room is carried up two storeys in height, and in the part away from the chief fireplace and ingle, a music gallery is contrived.

No pictures *hang* from the walls of the house, each painting having been done by Mr Hugh Wallis in a decorative manner either in or for its place. Many of us gather together a miscellaneous collection of pictures, some of which we admire critically and to most of which we are somewhat attached; yet merely to hang these round a room from a picture rail, however skilfully, is not to make of them satisfactory elements of decoration: they do not take their place in a complete scheme as elements of decoration should: they only too often disturb the harmonious effect the room might have had, and destroy its chance of being in itself a complete picture.

Yet I am very loath to believe that the enormous strides in realism we have made in modern times are all in a wrong direction, and am inclined to think that perhaps we should admit a greater degree of realism in pictures which we still regard as an element in decoration than many authorities would commend. Certainly some of our greatest painters, no matter what degree of realism they bring into their work, still (instinctively, it seems) maintain a decorative feeling which makes it fall easily into a scheme for a whole room. We have then only to find a place for such pictures where they can be relieved from that merely accidental or temporary look given by hanging from a picture rail, and to see that the colour scheme of each picture harmonises with that of the room in which it is placed, or, if necessary, adapt the colouring of the room to harmonise with the picture.

5

◇◇

Building in Relation to Site

In one or two houses already illustrated, notably in 'The Homestead' at Chesterfield and in 'Hilltop' at Caterham, one of the living rooms is large enough to fulfil any purpose to which it is likely to be put, and there are separate rooms for special uses. But in other houses it becomes necessary to contrive so that some of the space may be used for special occasions as well as for more general purposes. This arrangement is necessary when designing houses which, while they fulfil the requirements, and adapt themselves to the lives, of their occupants, are strictly limited as to size and cost.

'Glaed Hame' was designed for a man who from time to time would have large social gatherings in his house, but did not wish to build one room large enough for this purpose. Hence the arrangement whereby dining room, living room and hall can be thrown into one at need. These rooms are separated one from another by sliding doors. In one case these doors have wing walls to receive them; in the other, one door slides behind the seat and bookcases which are in the ingle and the second behind the piano. This arrangement is convenient in that it leaves no 'temporary' or unfinished look when the three rooms are thrown together, but provides a spacious and comfortable area for the entertainment of a number of people.

Perhaps the chief gain from this arrangement is to the members of the family. For them, there is the healthiness and freedom of living in a large room should they care to do so and the weather be suitable; yet if separate rooms for specific purposes are wanted, that can be easily managed. For instance, the dining room may be just closed off from the rest of the rooms while meals are being laid, taken and cleared away, so that the smell of food may not penetrate beyond it. The service from the butler's pantry and kitchen to the dining room may be accomplished without passing through the hall, in order to secure more complete isolation of the kitchen premises and privacy of the hall and living room.

And when does the weather in England make a large room undesirable? Possibly when it is of the very coldest, and in the absence of any heating apparatus to supplement the heat from open fires, a large room (especially when it has in it a staircase leading to rooms above) may be difficult to keep sufficiently warm. At these times it may be pleasant to shut off the hall and staircase.

58

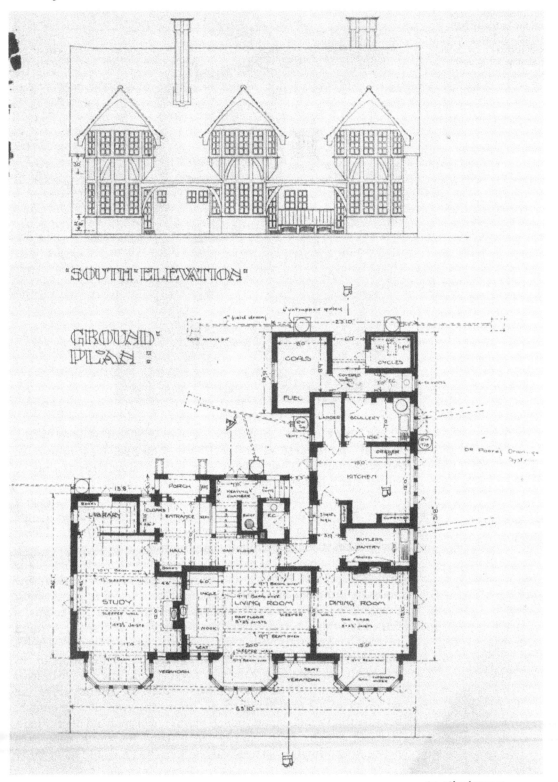

"SOUTH" ELEVATION"

GROUND"
PLAN"

26 'Glaed Hame',
Letchworth: ground floor
plan and south elevation

27 'Glaed Hame': view
from the entrance hall
through the living room to
the dining room with all
the sliding doors open

The large room at 'Glaed Hame' has two fireplaces, as have also the halls at 'The Homestead' and at 'Hilltop'. This I believe is unusual in America, but at 'Glaed Hame' the heating apparatus is only to supplement, not at all to take the place of, open fires.

The site of 'Glaed Hame' was indeed a specially easy one to design a house for. When placed to face due south the windows would command the best view and also a peep into the glade from which it partly takes its name; while the approach could be from the north, leaving all the pleasanter sides to be occupied by the windows of the principal rooms. Perhaps the chief difficulties arose from the necessity of having a verandah on the south side, where it was most desirable not to lose either sunshine or light from the rooms, a difficulty which constantly recurs for English architects. A south verandah is generally wished for in country houses, yet the architect cannot place any windows of importance under the roofs of his verandahs, except they are the windows of rooms intended to be used exclusively as cool rooms in hot weather. He cannot have the windows of general living rooms under the roof of a verandah, because this would impart to such rooms too dismal and depressing a character, so he must contrive to arrange his south verandahs between windows, in spaces where otherwise he would have either blank walls or windows of entirely secondary importance. At 'Glaed Hame' such spaces scarcely existed, so very careful consideration of the balance of advantages between the pleasantness of rooms and of the verandahs was necessary.

Perhaps one of the greatest advantages this house possesses is that of having no drain of any description below the surface of the ground. It is held that drainage only becomes dangerous when light and air are excluded therefrom. The drainage in this instance is carried from the sinks, lavatories and baths in open iron channels laid on the surface of the ground to a distance of a few yards from the house; thence in similar but perforated channels, it is distributed in various directions over the surface of the kitchen garden. Through the perforations it percolates into the surface soil, this being facilitated by broken stones laid in shallow trenches under the channels. The result is that the drainage never gets beyond the reach of the benign influence of light and air. The position of the channels can be changed occasionally if the surface soil in their neighbourhood becomes too saturated, but this is only necessary when the soil of the locality is rather unusually heavy. Earth closets are used. I fear such an arrangement for the disposal of drainage is not possible where houses are close together, and that town dwellers must continue to add the risks they run from less sanitary systems to the many other risks to which they are exposed and from which the country dweller is immune. Still, it does seem foolish that many from choice would subject themselves to the dangers of underground drains who might be free therefrom.

At a little distance from the outside walls at 'Glaed Hame' is an open channel of glazed earthenware which receives the rainwater, running into it from the roof by the customary downspouts. From this another channel similarly formed carries the water to a small pond in the garden; so even the rainwater is not allowed any chance of becoming a menace to health in underground drains, but is always open to observation and running in open channels which can be brushed out and cleaned with perfect ease as often as necessary.

It will be seen from the plans of 'The Coppice' that the conditions laid down by the site and by the client were similar to those at 'Glaed Hame'. Both houses, facing south, looked out over a beautiful pastoral landscape. The chief difference between the design is that the approach to 'The Coppice' is unavoidably from the east, whereas, as I have said, that to 'Glaed Hame' is from the north. At 'The Coppice' exceptional isolation of the kitchen premises was particularly desired, and a greater distance than is usual in a house of this size between the principal living rooms and the kitchen. It was the wish of the client to be quite out of range of the kitchen sounds and smells, and also that the servants should live more independent lives than they could if in closer proximity to the family.

The most definite determining factor in the plan for 'The Coppice'

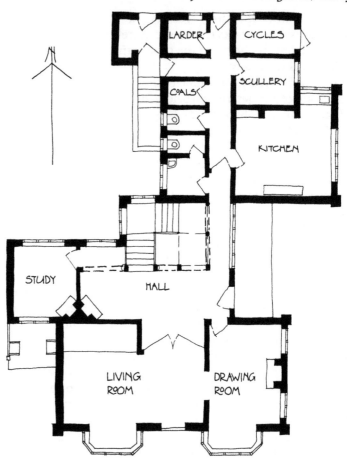

was a charming little wood which occupies the northwest corner of
the plot of ground. The right thing obviously was that the house
should surround this on two sides, that the owner might enjoy
glimpses into the cool recesses of this wood from the windows they
would constantly pass or sit near. I tried to gain these peeps into the
wood as well as the outlook to the south for the principal rooms, but
found this to be impossible except by means of a plan too straggling to
be compatible with economy in building, with consideration of the
labour involved in the working of the house, and with the
dimensions of the plot of ground. So I was obliged to rest contented
with windows in the hall and study looking into the wood; one of
these windows in the hall was placed where it created vistas from the
principal rooms terminating in the wood, and the kitchen wing was
so planned that the land between the wood and the house did not
partake of the character of a backyard but became a little secluded
garden enclosed by the house on two sides and the wood on a third.

So it is with an architect's work generally. It resolves itself into
balancing advantages, and his critics generally discover advantages

29 'The Coppice': exterior from the south-east

30 'The Coppice': view across the hall showing the framing of the stair

he has failed to secure and disregard those alternative ones he has thought greater and therefore preferred to gain.

To return to the points of similarity between the plans of 'Glaed Hame' and 'The Coppice'. Both these houses have a room set aside for taking meals in, but often a charming effect can be obtained if the dining room is so reduced in dimensions that it becomes a mere dining recess, opening off the living rooms, but there is the

31 'Little Molewood',
Hertford: ground floor plan

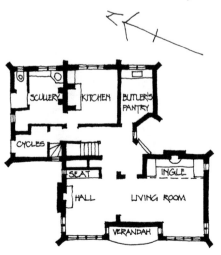

32 'Little Molewood':
exterior from the west
showing the symmetry of
the façade of the main
block and the junction with
the service wing

disadvantage that the dining recess is not well adapted to other purposes than that of taking meals, and again there is the inconvenience that those who serve cannot pass all round the table. Such recesses should have seats fixed against the walls, and comfortably contrived for those who sit at the table. It should be possible to lay and clear the table in such a recess, and serve without entering any other part of the living room, just as in the dining room at 'Glaed Hame'.

In the designs for 'Little Molewood' at Hertford, the two principal rooms are divided by large double doors in such a way that at will the two become one. At 'Glaed Hame' and 'The Coppice' the dining room is placed where east windows are possible; this brings the morning sun with its cheering effects into the room where breakfast is taken. At 'Little Molewood' there is no dining room, but an east window is assigned to the living room.

6

◇-◇

Air and Light in Buildings

Let us at this stage consider the advantages and disadvantages of high and low rooms. We are apt to take it for granted that high rooms are necessarily in every way more desirable; we presuppose that they are more healthy because they provide more air space than do low rooms; but it does not always strike us that it would be well to take each case on its own merits and see whether at times this additional space in the height might not better be added to the width and length of the rooms.

Artistically, most rooms in small houses suffer from too great height in proportion to their width and length, yet the charm resulting from carrying one room (say a hall) considerably higher than any of the others is as indisputable as the fact that both the high and the low rooms gain by the contrast.

In terrace houses and where land is very valuable, air space can be more cheaply gained by increase in height than in width and length, and must therefore be so gained. Again, in terrace houses each room generally can have windows in only one of its walls, hence these windows must be carried high enough to enable the light therefrom to reach to the back of the room.

If we are to derive health and pleasure from the time we spend in our homes we can hardly attach too great importance to this bringing of the light and sunshine into the very hearts of them. In houses such as we are considering, most of the rooms are in positions where it would be possible to have windows in more than one wall, so height in most of them is not necessary to gain light and sunshine in all parts. However, in each there is generally one room on the ground floor so placed that it could only have windows in one wall, so in each of the houses this room is carried up two storeys. 'Balnagowan' and 'The Gables' each have big south windows which are carried up the full height of these rooms. In 'Balnagowan' particularly one appreciates the enormous gain of allowing the sunshine and light by this means to stream into the innermost parts of the house. This house is built on a site which falls very rapidly indeed from north to south, so that the ground is level with the ground floor on the north side and with the basement floor on the south side. This made it possible to place the

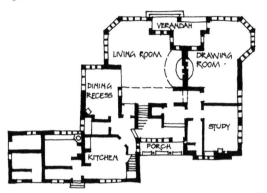

33 'The Gables', Harrogate: ground floor plan

34 'The Gables': the ingle-nook in the main living room

servant's bedroom, the laundry and some other rooms in the basement, in accordance with a common custom in Scotland, without their having any of the unhealthiness or other disadvantages of rooms below the ground. It will not be necessary to point out that in these houses, as in former ones illustrated, attempts have been made to reinstate the hall or houseplace, and make it the most important and homelike room in each house, the room in which the family chiefly lives. Also it will be seen that there is a slight similarity in the general arrangement of these houses, but that each takes as simply and directly as possible the form dictated by the site and local conditions and the requirements of the client.

35 'Balnagowan',
Edinburgh: ground floor
plan

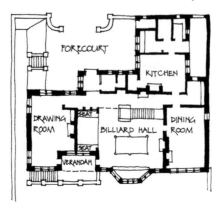

36 'Balnagowan': south
façade. The tall bay window
lights the double-height
living room.

7

◇◇◇

Building for Professional People

We have considered somewhat the way in which the personalities and habits of those who are to occupy a house should influence its planning. We have seen also how questions as to the degree and manner of 'entertaining' proposed must affect its arrangement, but up to this point in the examples used in illustration we have not perhaps noticed how far the client's profession may exercise a direct influence over a plan. So far the client's profession or business has scarcely controlled the planning more than have his hobbies and interests; only inasmuch as it determines whether he shall be a studious, a quiet or busy man and shall or shall not be constantly interviewing or entertaining has it been taken into consideration at all.

The house of the general medical practitioner must be to some extent his place of business. To separate his home life from his professional life in the way members of some other professions are able to is not possible. He is liable to be called upon at any hour of the day or night, so just as his home life and professional life cannot be separated, neither can the buildings where each is carried on. His house must then be one in which both lives may be easily and smoothly carried on together, each interfering with the other as little as possible. To secure this, patients must be able to enter the waiting rooms and surgery without intrusion into any domestic regions, which at the same time must be easily accessible. That the distance between the kitchen and the entrance should be short is even more important in the house of a general medical practitioner than in other houses, for it will more frequently have to be traversed. The difficulty of securing this is increased when the requirements of the case necessitate two entrances, one for the inmates of the house and their visitors and one to the surgery and the consulting room. In this case the entrances should not be near together, or the object in having two would probably be defeated. Hence the kitchen must come about halfway between the entrances; also the traffic from the kitchen to either door must not pass where it could exercise a disturbing influence upon the quietude of the house, but must be aloof from the scenes of the household life.

There are perhaps one or two specific points in the house at

37 Doctor's house at Minehead. The surgery entrance is located under the archway on the right, well away from the family entrance.

Minehead which may be of interest. Beautiful stone being plentiful and inexpensive in the locality, all the fireplaces were built of it. The special form given to the ingle in the living room resulted from the client's wish to have a view from here of a fine wooded hill which rose to the north of the site and was one of the prides and pleasures of the people thereabouts. Not wishing to break the line of the house front as seen from the road by bringing the living room forward enough to secure this, an outside seat recess was formed, and in this recess the three-sided bay from which the 'North Hill' could be seen. Hitherto I have avoided laying stress upon this question of securing pleasant vistas within our houses, fearing that such considerations might be thought fanciful by some. I am, however, so convinced that they are really essential that I must run the risk of being held to attach too much weight thereto. Vistas of one sort or another there will be, and instead of being one of the most fruitful sources of charm, and perhaps of increasing the feeling of spaciousness in a house, they will, if unconsidered, only give us a shut-in feeling, and a sense of something indefinably unsatisfactory.

8

◇-◇

True Economy in Architecture

One of the definite requirements which an architect should welcome most heartily is the necessity to consider real economy, for not only will this increase his chances of artistic success, but it will give him an added satisfaction in his work; it will increase his chances of artistic success by tending towards that element of simplicity and directness so necessary, and lessening his risk of falling into the vulgarity almost inseparable from superfluity.

Perhaps it is in engineering work that we see most clearly how grace results from true economy of material and labour. When we can feel that the strength of each part is adequate and that nothing is unnecessary, an element of beauty is introduced into the most utilitarian works, for which all artists are grateful, and by which they profit.

Though less easily discovered in architectural work, this element of grace resulting from economy is none the less necessary to success. The economy the architect should seek will be that which is to be reached by increasing his skill in planning and in the use of materials; it will never be that which is arrived at by the use of materials less fitted to the purposes to which they are put, or methods of construction which are quicker but less permanent.

The imperative necessity of constantly reiterating and demonstrating what is right in methods of designing is brought home to me again and again, and I must perforce comply with it. If there are any people who think it an already universally recognised fact that architects should plan to secure practical and sensible requirements of comfort and convenience, and out of these gain balanced and overall expression, let them observe the flat denials of this there are on every hand in our modern buildings.

They will find very few buildings of today which have really been designed from the inside out. Some may feel it unnecessary to labour this point, and I only wish they were right. Mr C. F. A. Voysey once suggested that 'architecture was not the art of fitting the requirements of a Borough Council into a Greek Temple or Roman Bath', and the principle thus enunciated is one which needs driving home.

Those who feel the beauties of certain proportions and relations of parts in a design are tempted to endeavour to put these first and good planning second, and we must be content to 'hammer away' until this point of view is overcome, for it never will produce buildings of beautiful proportions or any structure that will ring true. Start if you will with attempts to evade or falsify the facts, or with the desire for a particular effect unrelated to them; facts are stubborn things: one by one they will crop up and in the end deprive you even of the effect for which you have been willing to sacrifice so much.

Can it be doubted that the honest expression of a well thought out plan, based on considerations of health, happiness, convenience and comfort must needs result in more comeliness than can be compassed where the first thought is for the proportioning of a façade?

9

◇◇◇

Relation of Ornament to Construction

It is extremely difficult to be sure that we are not using as decoration that which appears to be construction, and is not. But to do this always imparts a subtle indefinite sense of insincerity, and want of dignity, if nothing more; hence the importance of being so strongly imbued with the spirit of truth that the slightest violation of it causes pain.

Let us try by further illustration drawn from the use of the column to make clearer the principle we are considering. The column is primarily constructional. The ancients in hot climates erected columns at a distance from the walls of their temples to secure coolness within, and to give shade where shade was scanty and precious. These columns supported the roofs, which were brought over onto them, so preventing the sunlight from falling on to the walls. The architectural effect was magnificent. So attempts to reproduce it were made in sunless climes, where the absence of reason for it, based upon its practical advantages, produced an element of falseness, and disillusion followed.

That less of the none too abundant light might be excluded from subsequent buildings the wall was brought forward up to the columns. These latter therefore lost their function as supports; so a stronger element of falseness was introduced, bringing with it greater disappointment in the effect produced. Eventually a form of building was reached which is ever present with us today; one in which columns, three-quarter columns, half columns and pilasters with their entablatures seem to have been 'clapped on' to the face of the structures, though striving to appear an integral part of them. An uncomfortable feeling follows such as could never arise from the use of pure ornament as decoration.

Mr Norman Shaw has connected two wings, which occur in the upper part of the Piccadilly front of the Piccadilly Hotel, by a screen formed of columns supporting an entablature. Merely to glance up at this brings a feeling of calm and tranquillity to many amidst the bustle and turmoil of life in the street below. We must admit that numerous other instances could be given of elements originally constructional, used beautifully as decoration, and not take the position that what was constructional should never be used as decoration pure and simple, even though we hold it better to use what is always pure ornament when we want decoration.

Where then may we find the differences between the insincere buildings which jar on us, and this of Mr Norman Shaw's or the many others which furnish instances of the successful decorative use of much which first came into existence to fulfil the demands of construction? Shall we have found it if we discover that in those we admire, whatever was once construction and is now used as decoration is unmistakably so used, giving the observer no chance of confusing the one with the other? It would seem as if pure decoration should proclaim itself and claim a right to exist as such, as admittedly decoration pure and simple.

There would also seem to be many degrees of architectural insincerity, ranging from the deliberate lie told with intent to deceive (as when wood is made to simulate stone vaulting) through shams such as imitation ruins, then through the many uses of effects without legitimate causes, to confusion finally between construction and decoration. I am inclined to believe that the way to safeguard against the taint of untruth is to think first of what is necessary to a building, necessary to enable it to fulfil its functions, necessary to its strength and stability, its water-tightness and durability; and only then how we may use to the full decorative qualities inherent in the conditions. Finally (having in imagination swept all else away) we should allow nothing to be added which cannot show an indisputable right to exist because it is beautiful and proclaims this as the reason for its being. For we must always remember that a purely ornamental feature can only base a valid claim to existence on the ground of its own beauty.

The house at Rugby brings up many problems in addition to those we have already considered; mainly, those which arise when designing houses which have a limited frontage, and must be sandwiched in between other buildings. During a discussion which once followed a lecture of mine, an architect said that the real difficulties of planning only began with such a house. I think in taking this view he overlooked much in the work of his profession worthy of being taken more seriously; still it is true that with the additional limitations entailed by a restricted site further care and skill are required of the architect, while some loss of comfort and convenience is inevitable.

But if a site such as we are now considering limits the architect in some directions, it opens up for him a wider field for the exercise of his faculties in others. It gives him opportunities for considering his work in relation to that of others, which are lacking in designing a house to stand alone. His own work has more unmistakably to take its place as part of a whole, that whole being the street in which it is placed. This broadening of his view can scarcely fail to have a beneficial influence upon his work, the bigger conception giving

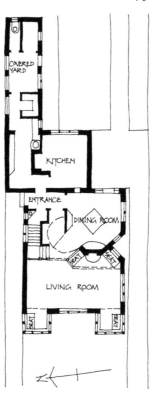

38 Vause House, Rugby:
ground floor plan

39 Vause House: living
room showing the 'free'
arrangement of the interior
behind the strict symmetry
of the street façade

breadth to it. Hitherto, often the architect has thought only of the
appearance of his own building. Sometimes he has yielded to the
temptation to make the surrounding buildings look mean, as he
confesses by the way he treats them in his perspective drawings. But
when every architect designing a town building realises that his
design is part of the whole street, and that he personally is responsible
for a share of the whole, then not only will the gain in civic beauty be

enormous but the individual work of each man will appear to be the greatest possible advantage.

The site at Rugby is not really a narrow one: there is good passageway on either side of the house. But even here the importance of dispelling the cramped and airless feeling usually associated with the interiors of houses with restricted frontages should be our first consideration. By devoting the whole ground floor of the house to one large room, and not excluding entirely from it the space which would usually be shut off into the entrance hall or that occupied by the staircase, a feeling of space and openness was at least secured, and in addition, vistas were opened up.

There was greater openness on the south than on the north side. At any time there was the danger that the neighbour might erect a fence on this north boundary, which would block the south ground floor windows, diagonal windows in both dining and living rooms were contrived, so that the outlook could not at any time be completely obscured.

10

Architecture Adjusted to Space

The order in which we have been considering the various houses illustrated, namely that of diminishing cost, brings us now to a group of medium-sized houses; they are one and all detached houses, though some were designed for plots with very narrow frontages.

The doctor's house at Bradford in Yorkshire has a very restricted site, bounded on three sides by roads. When designing a house for such a site, our first consideration should be not to lose the great advantage of being on a corner plot. From it, views should be obtained not only up and down the one street, but down the branch streets also, and if at the crossing of two streets, then both up and down the crossing street as well. To secure these advantages it has been customary to furnish such houses with corner oriels, angle bays or turrets. The building of these has been attended with constructional difficulties, particularly in roofing them successfully, and in projecting them from the walls.

To overcome such difficulties the builder's greatest power and ingenuity have been exerted, and, as so often happens in architectural work, this conquest of difficulties when striving for a reasonable and sensible object, has been most fruitful of charm. This charm has been appreciated, and attempts made to reproduce it, often by those who have lost sight of its cause. So corner bays, oriels and turrets have

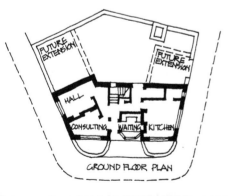

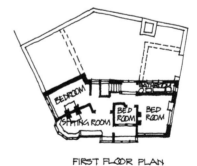

40 Doctor's house at Bradford: ground and first floor plans

41 House at Westcliffe-on-
Sea: ground floor plan

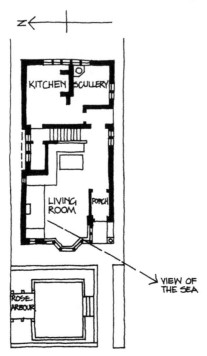

come to be recognised forms of corner treatment, and to be added to buildings merely as ornaments. We even find them so designed that views therefrom are not obtainable in more than one direction. This is another example of features which should fulfil a definite purpose wrongly used as ornament alone.

I have spoken of the desirability of giving each room its proper 'direction', should it not be possible to secure this for a room which has a corner window, without the necessity of moving from the part of the room one would naturally occupy, to gain the advantages the oriel offers? Hence the fireplace and centre of the life in the room should be placed where those round it profit freely by the bay.

Perhaps enumerating what is most important to consider in the design for a small detached house on a narrow fronted plot may prove useful, and result in a list we could apply to any such house. The assumption being that the house on either side will be close upon it, we must only count upon having staircase, larder, bathroom and similar windows in our side walls, or supplementary and very secondary windows of kitchen, sitting rooms and bedrooms. All important windows must come on one of the other two sides. Of these two sides, one, either that toward the road or that away from it, will be the pleasanter, because of prospect or aspect or a combination of the two, and the first thing to be done is to decide upon this pleasanter side as the one for our principal room. Having seen which is the pleasanter side of the house we must appreciate that its frontage is far too precious and limited for any of it to be devoted to the front door or to windows of lobbies. We must next see that the roof is absolutely simple. If it consists of more than a single span we must ascertain why, and whether there has been a compensating gain commensurate with the loss of simplicity and space and the additional cost entailed.

If the hall is to be used as a sitting room, we should see that the traffic from room to room, or to the stairs or front door does not cross it, but is confined to a part devoted thereto. Particularly must we notice that the cold stream of air which pours down the staircase from the colder rooms above it to the warmer ones below, is not directed toward the occupants of the hall, but away from the regions of the fireplace, principal windows and any other parts of the room in which people would naturally sit.

A window should be placed in such a position that it will ventilate the upper landing; for vitiated air is apt to accumulate there when it rises from the rooms below, and if it is not carried outside it finds its way into the rooms above. While speaking of landings, I should say that where space permits of wide open landings and corridors they greatly add to the pleasantness of a house, but in one such as we are considering no space should be devoted to them, which by care in planning, could have been included in the rooms.

Finally we should see that in all bedrooms there are good places for the beds, mirrors, dressing tables and washstands. It is not uncommon for a whole plan, which is otherwise good, to be entirely remodelled, because one of the bedrooms comes out with no good place for the bed, though perhaps a spacious room.

11

◇◇◇

The Relation of Houses and Furniture

We now come to the point at which I can best attempt to make clear a principle applicable to all houses, though I have avoided speaking of it until arriving at that type of house in which it is most systematically neglected. This principle is, that our aim should be to so arrange that all sides of a house are equally satisfying to look upon. There is generally no reason why this should not be the case, but it seldom is so, because we start out wrongly. We assume that a house must have front, sides and back, that we must 'make our best show in front', that the sides may be less nice and the back must be necessarily to some extent unpleasant, if not a little squalid. We bring this about at the outset by failing to include under our main roof some required accommodation, such as coal place, cycle house, a place for the ashbin, or a shed, so one or more of these have to be put up as outbuildings, with the result that all windows on the sides on which they have been erected, look out upon them, and the rooms to which these windows belong become at once back rooms. The appearance of that side of the house is being spoiled. Clearly it must be the height of folly to spoil the outlook from our own windows by putting up buildings which obstruct and disfigure the view and would have cost less had they been planned under the same roof as the house.

To take the house called 'Letchworth' at Horsted Keynes, in Sussex, as an example. I suppose it would generally be assumed, without consideration, that either toward the road or away from the road must be the back of this house and one of these sides necessarily be spoiled. Now 'Letchworth' was on a curious and interesting site. It was in an orchard skirted by the main road on the southwest, but the best of the outlook was northeast down the orchard and away to the hills, and the land fell rapidly in that direction. As the house had to be approached from the southwest and the principal rooms had to have windows looking out in this direction as well as out to the northeast, or they would lose either sun or view, it was even more important than is generally the case that neither of these sides should have the appearance of being the back.

But to other causes as well as these must be attributed the somewhat unusual form given to the plan for this house. One was the wish to fit it in among the trees of the orchard, cutting down as few as

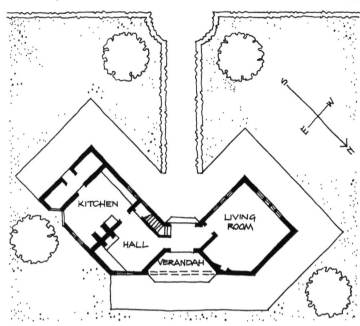

possible and retaining those which could least well be spared, while
contriving that the house should not be overshadowed by them.
Another was that the verandah, stoep, or garden room, while it must
be away from the road and overlook the orchard, should not give a
sunless impression. After the early morning, this latter would have
been the case had it not been made possible for those using the
verandah to be conscious of and to feel the effect of the sunshine on
the southwest side of the house through the glass doors which
enclosed the verandah on this side.

Perhaps the chief interest which attaches to the illustrations given
in this chapter is that they furnish examples of houses which prove
that simple furnishing may be done less expensively by having
furniture designed with and for the house, and as far as possible made
by the builder, than by buying from the shops. When the furniture is
designed for and with the house the owner has just what he wants
and requires, and nothing beyond this. Suppose a man wants a
sideboard. Perhaps he simply wants a table top on which to set things
down, a drawer for the tablecloths and table napkins, and a cupboard
for cruets, decanters, salt cellars, etc. If he sets out to purchase these in
the shops, to get what he wants he is almost certain to be obliged to
pay in addition for something he does *not* want. If he has not to put up
with a little meaningless fence of turned balusters on his sideboard,
he is sure to have to try and smile while paying for a broken pediment
or a mirror, some recesses for ornaments, bracketed shelves, a brass
rail or some other things he would rather be without, in order that he
may get those things which he does require. If his furniture is being

43 'Letchworth': entrance
detail from an original
perspective by Parker

made for and with his house, just what he requires and nothing more
will be provided. If the architect knows in advance what will be
wanted, a recess or other place will be contrived for the fitting in the
building, without adding to its cost, but reducing the cost of making
the sideboard by providing it with back and ends. What is true of a
side table applies with equal force to wardrobes, writing desks,
washstands, dressing tables, bookcases and shelves, drawers, dressers, seats and cupboards, and almost all the furnishing of a house;
they may be fitted into the structure much more cheaply than they
can be procured separate from it. There is a difference between the
traditions which obtain among cabinet-makers and joiners. While
the work of the latter is generally stronger, it has not that degree of

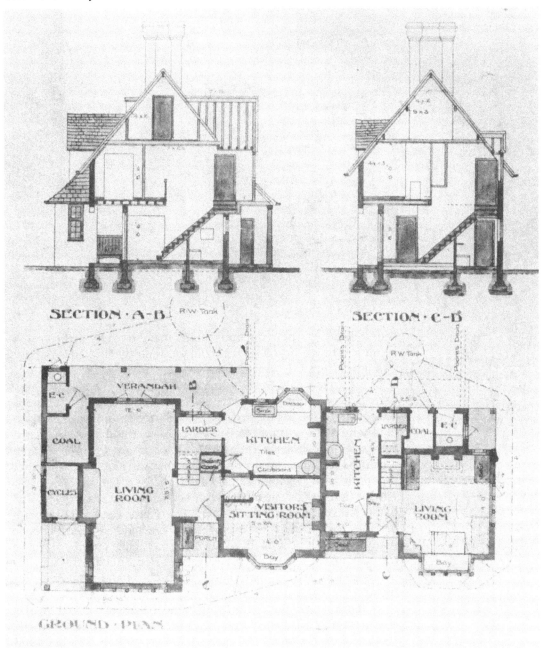

SECTION·A-B   R W Tank

SECTION·C-D

GROUND·PLAN

mechanical finish given to it, that the work of the former has. For my own part, I would rather pay for good workmanship than for mechanical finish. My sympathies are with the joiners' traditions, and I am glad that they tend to keep down the price of their work. My experience has been that the cost of furniture made with and for the house may be reduced in price to an extent which far more than

44 'Laneside', Letchworth: ground plan and cross-sections. The left-hand house of this semi-detached pair was, briefly, Raymond Unwin's home before he moved to Hampstead. The right-hand house later became Barry Parker's home and was much extended.

counterbalances the reductions which may be made in the cost of furniture shown in the shops, owing to their manufacture in large quantities from the same design.

Of the artistic gain from having everything designed for its place, perhaps I need not speak here, but I must enlarge on the practical advantages of having a place designed for everything. There are few of us who do not at times find it depressing to think how much time we waste in looking for things. I do not mean only the time spent in looking for things we never find, or only find after long searching, but time lost by not laying our hands on what we want at once. Now when a house and its furniture have been designed as a whole, some of this loss of time can be prevented. Everything can have that place designed for it which is the most obvious and handy, there will not be many places where it might equally well have been put; there will be the place for the housewife's sewing things, for the children's toys, for books and for writing materials, for pamphlets and magazines, for music, tobacco, and so forth.

An interest attaching to the living room of 'Laneside' at Letchworth comes from its being the first room illustrated in this series of articles (with the exception of the living room in 'Hilltop' at Caterham) which has the brickwork of the walls left unplastered. Here they have been whitewashed, but at 'Hilltop' they were left in the natural red colour of the brickwork. The possible economy effected by eliminating the plaster was not the only consideration. That the texture, surface and character of brickwork is more interesting and artistic than the flat monotony of plaster can scarcely be denied. The effort we make to regain some of the qualities our walls have lost by being plastered, by covering them with first one kind of wall-paper or hanging and then another, would indicate this. The attempt to make use of the texture of the brickwork as a decoration, because one inherent in the materials used in construction, was surely on the right lines and had also the advantage of a surface which is not liable to injury from the slightest knock, as is that of plaster.

12

Interesting Placing of Suburban Houses

Taken together, a number of houses which stand detached or semi-detached in the middle of a small building plot constitute perhaps the most difficult problem of the domestic architect – that of creating with them any good collective effect. Each of the houses in a row of suburban building plots may be individually delightful, but the total result a most unsatisfactory effect. In few terrace houses are we so insistently made conscious of our neighbours as we are in a suburban house standing in its own little plot. The garden of such a house seldom amounts to more than a small strip in front and behind, still smaller strips at either side, all too small to be dealt with in any way that can produce a pleasing effect. A great deal too of the dismal, forbidding aspect of our suburbs is due to the endless line of fencing. It is seldom that we find two adjacent plots with a similar treatment of boundaries. Here we have an oak fence, there a privet, a briar, a barbed wire, or stone. If we could erase most of these boundaries and create something akin to the fenceless suburbs of many American towns we should have done much toward bestowing a pleasing appearance on our English suburban streets.

Since the house that the domestic architect will most frequently be commissioned to design will be detached or semi-detached on the customary suburban building plot, it behoves us to consider suggestions for overcoming the difficulties in such planning. Dismissing as a stupid convention the dictate that the principal windows of a house should always overlook the road, whatever their aspect, we find that the side elevations present our chief difficulties. From the side windows we look straight across to those in our neighbours' side walls, and it is this that makes us so conscious of neighbours, and they so much more 'upon us' in a suburban house than in a terrace house.

At 'St Brighid's' no windows look straight across at the neighbouring houses, and even for the least advantageously placed window a much more open, pleasant and sunny outlook has been secured than could have been given to any side windows opposed to the side walls of the neighbouring houses. The neighbours also gain by having no windows looking directly at them. In fact, it practically amounts to

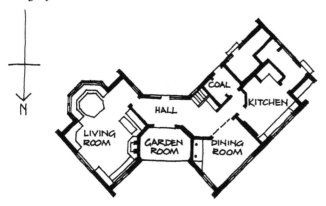

46 'St Brighid's',
Letchworth: ground floor
plan

this house having three sides which face the garden (the pleasantest, sunniest aspect), instead of one.

To obtain the charm of a vista right through the house and down the garden as one approached the front door on the north side was one of the main factors in producing the form of the plan used. The difficulties in designing this house would have been greatly lessened had the client required fewer bedrooms or more ground floor accommodation.

As will be seen from the drawing, the house was practically furnished when it left the builder's hands. In most of the bedrooms, wardrobes, cupboards, drawers, dressing tables and washstands were built under the slope of the roof where the headroom was not great enough to allow anyone to stand. The kitchen was fitted practically all the way round with seats, cupboards, drawers, dressers, etc. Bookshelves, cupboards, cabinets, seats, etc., occupied almost all the wall space in the living room, as will be seen from the photograph. Anything required on the dining table can be put on to the sideboard in the dining room through a serving door on the kitchen side of it, and all this furniture was included in the cost stated at the beginning.

The 'adzed' beams in the ceiling of the living room at 'St Brighid's' have been painted white. Had they been left dark, say the natural colour of the wood, the effect, with the white walls and the room a low one, would have been that these beams would have been too insistent. A dark ceiling in a room whose walls are equally dark may have a very pleasant effect; or a dark ceiling in a very high room, even with light walls, may look well; but a dark ceiling in a room as low as this one would assert itself too much. As a matter of fact, the slight play of light and shade on the tooled surfaces of these beams is not lost at all by their being whitened. The colour scheme throughout the whole house is white for walls, ceilings and all fireplaces. Touches of bright peacock blues, greens and purples in rugs and upholstery, and dark oak furniture have a pleasing effect in conjunction with the ceilings and walls showing in the one case the beams and joists, and in the other the texture of brickwork.

47 'Briarside', Letchworth:
ground floor plan

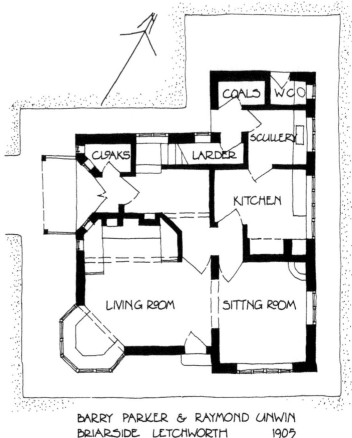

BARRY PARKER & RAYMOND UNWIN
BRIARSIDE LETCHWORTH   1905

48 'Briarside', Letchworth:
the living room

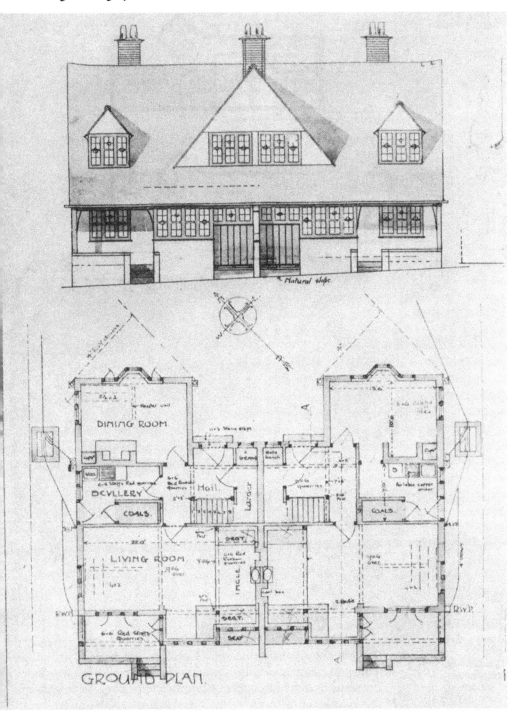

49 Semi-detached houses at Hampstead Garden Suburb: ground and first floor plan

50 'The Cottage', Newton, near Cambridge: ground floor plan

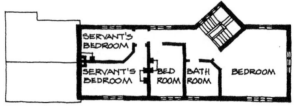

FIRST FLOOR PLAN

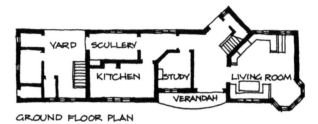

GROUND FLOOR PLAN

51 'The Cottage': view from the west. The underlying geometrical order of the design is hinted at in the division of the façade into three equal bays by the expression of the timber frame in the centre.

The interior of 'Briarside' has cream as the basis of its colour scheme and cream quarry tiles (unglazed) are used for the fireplaces.

The semi-detached houses at Hampstead are given as an example of those designed with their principal windows away from the road, because they thus obtain a more pleasant and sunny outlook, but at the same time they are planned to secure another window overlooking the road.

Because it had proved itself to produce a very warm and damp-resisting wall, costing less than would any other in that neighbourhood, I revived a local tradition and built the walls of the house at Newton, near Cambridge, of sun-dried clay batts. In size they were eighteen inches by nine inches by six inches, and they were formed in tempered clay mixed with straw.

13

◇◆◇

Buildings Suggested by the Site

Two things have made me realise that, though constant reference has been made to the influence which the effort to secure sunshine has had upon the planning of the houses illustrated, no reasons have yet been given for attaching so much importance to sunlight. As the search for sunlight has largely dominated the development of the plans for the two houses at Letchworth which are given here, it may be interesting to quote a statement in a recent issue of *The Lancet*, to the effect that architects 'do not yet fully appreciate the question of direct rays of sunlight, that a room into which no sunlight ever penetrates can never be a healthy habitation'.

Apart from the actual direct health-giving power of sunlight, a room made cheerful and bright by it has the same effect upon us which beauty in our surroundings has. To quote again from *The Lancet*: 'Joy is essentially a wholesome feeling. Beauty is preventive and curative medicine; it helps to make us happy and therefore in good health, while if unfortunately sickness has invaded our system we are much more likely to find the necessary vitality to recover in the contemplation of things that are graceful, pleasing and inspiring than in the contemplation of drab ugliness.'

From Mr Stanley Parker's house at Letchworth the finest view is out to the west, so the living room must occupy the southwest corner of the house to secure this view. The studio, of course, should have a north window, but my client, wishing also to enjoy the western view from this room, was willing to sacrifice a little of the efficiency of the room, as a studio, for a window looking west. He also wished for a south window in the kitchen, and was fortunately able to arrange his menage in such a way as to minimise the objections to this, valuing as he did the purifying effect of sunshine more highly than any avoidance of inconvenience arising from a superfluity of it.

The house was in a very exposed situation, so that much of the wall was built with greater thickness than is usual in a house of this character. It was of brick covered with roughcast, whitewashed with Russian tallow mixed in the whitewash to render it more damp-resisting and durable.

The window frames were cast in concrete, reinforced, and whitewashed as are the walls. Of all kinds of windows the sash is the

52 Stanley Parker's house, Letchworth: view from the north

53 Living room at Stanley Parker's house. The unadorned construction is fully expressed in conformity with Arts and Crafts principles.

most liable to defects arising from shrinking, warping and decaying wood, because it is built up of a greater number of comparatively thin and small timbers than any other; it is therefore most costly in repairs, upkeep and painting; it also rattles more than any other, and gives trouble from jamming and getting out of order, and owing to its weights, pulleys, cords and beads it is far more complicated in construction. Wood casement windows are freer from these defects, but metal casements in stone or concrete are freest. These latter have the additional advantage over both of the former that in them the glass, in such lights as are not required to open, is let directly into grooves in the stone or concrete, still further tending to reduce the defects I have been enumerating. The only advantage that a sash window has over the casement is that it may be opened a little at the top for ventilation at times when the windows otherwise cannot conveniently be kept open. An equivalent advantage may, however, be obtained with a casement window if one or more top panes are made to open in addition to the casement opening as a whole.

The other house at Letchworth (in Cashio Lane), illustrated, was built upon a site which dictated a very special plan. The client wished to have a window in the living room looking west, out on the road which passed the house. The finest view was out east, but on the north was an orchard into which it seemed a pity not to obtain a peep from the living room. This room had necessarily also to have windows on the south. To gain all these advantages with reasonable compactness of plan was the problem. To do this the living room had to be on the east side of the house, and to be thrown out enough to get north and south windows, and the west window had to be contrived between the other rooms and overlooking the porch.

A house somewhat similar in general scheme to the foregoing is the one designed for a site near Rochdale in Lancashire, and the illustrations here given show at a glance how much more compact and four-square a house may be when the conditions laid down by the site are favourable, and when compactness and squareness do not entail a sacrifice of greater advantages owing to the relations of approach, aspect and prospect. These latter two houses taken together illustrate how that balance of advantages, which it is ever the architect's business to watch, cause him sometimes to forego those of squareness and simplicity of roofing, legitimately seizing the opportunity afforded for more picturesque and varied roof lines and grouping, which would be false and wrong if introduced for their own sake.

As soon as the designer can see that the purposes and conditions he is designing to fulfil have ceased to be his inspiration and have come to be tiresome and irksome to him, he must beware, for his attitude of mind is one in which the best work cannot be done. If, in order to make it take a form he wishes it to take, he causes what he is designing to fulfil the purposes for which it is intended one whit less well than might have been, he is in sore danger of artistic failure. Flagrant examples of such failure are not easy to find because the public will not tolerate them, but examples of partial failure from this cause we have on every hand, especially in our household furniture. How much of this seems grudgingly to provide every little useful accommodation fitted into a compilation based on curious ideas of balanced parts and proportions. If it is difficult to see into a drawer

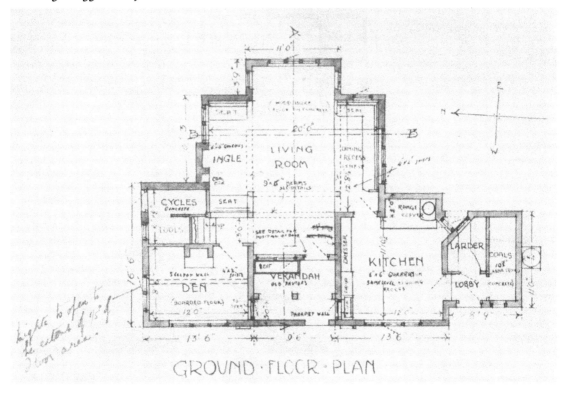

GROUND · FLOOR · PLAN

54 House in Cashio Lane,
Letchworth: ground floor
plan from original working
drawing

55 House in Cashio Lane:
view from the west

56 Project for a cottage at
Rochdale: ground floor plan

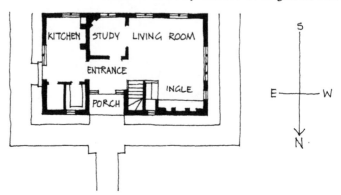

57 Project for a cottage at
Rochdale: entrance façade

58 Project for a cottage at
Rochdale: living room
interior

because something projects out over it the public will decline it. If the entrance into a cupboard is awkwardly placed, to avoid some loss of the designer's cherished conception, the public will see through this and ask for convenience instead of display; but the designer gets the better of the public by leaving out that drawer and cupboard altogether, and they cheerfully buy his balanced and proportioned compilation of inanities without realising how much more accommodation and convenience they might have had within the space it will occupy. Or the designer sinks still lower and palms off something worse on to a public not over-sensitive to sincerity or falseness in art. He causes the brackets or mouldings which apparently support something above the drawer and which come in the way of those who want to see into the drawer to move either with the drawer or with what is above them. His pilasters which are apparently important constructional parts of his compilation, but really come where they prevent his placing the cupboard doors in the convenient position, he attaches *to* the cupboard doors so that they move with them.

Before beginning to design anything always make a clear list of all requirements, then most vigorously ask at every stage as you proceed, even when the minutest details are reached, *why* do I include this or that? Is it simply because it is customary? If so, is there any real foundation or sober reason for it? Sometimes we shall find that what appears to be a meaningless convention has a foundation in true convenience, just as we often find that much which is apparently groundless in etiquette and conventional politeness and propriety has a basis in good feeling and consideration for others. But on the other hand the comfortable sophistry that, because almost universal, a custom must have advantages we do not see, is responsible for the perpetuation of many absurdities.

14

Symmetry in Building: The Result of Sincerity

It is not merely that a quiet dignity, a serenity and sense of sincerity will almost always be the natural outcome of building to express and fulfil definite sensible purposes, and to secure real advantages; but symmetry and balance will almost inevitably result – such symmetry and balance moreover as seems to elude those who definitely make it their object. Perhaps few things will impress more forcibly one who arranges rooms so as to gain the most for the occupants than the tendency the rooms evince to fall into a symmetrical and balanced scheme.

We have an instinct that there is something inherently right in the symmetrical arrangement of buildings. This we find grows in strength as we strive after sensible arrangement; and symmetry so arrived at will probably have a feeling of inevitability unattainable where balance of parts has been regarded as of the first importance.

Mr Alfred Gotch in his admirable book, 'The Growth of the English House', gives some most striking anachronisms produced in the eighteenth century by designing formal façades in accordance with measurements and rules of proportion, and then trying to fit to them the required accommodation. These methods have produced results almost as unhappy as the striving after the picturesque in later times. Mr Gotch instances a house in which 'the windows of the attic storey are in the frieze of the entablature that encompasses the building' and says, 'This would allow a width of from three to four feet by a height which could only be measured by inches for the windows of rooms of considerable area, a complete sacrifice of internal comfort for the sake of external effect.'

He goes on to an instance worse, relating to which Kent complaisantly said, 'the lodging rooms for servants receive their light from the hall', and another in which 'they are lighted from the roof where hidden from observation'. All this done to allow an entablature to come where the attic windows should have come. Some offices made five or six times as large as there is any sense in having them, and others cramped to almost impossible dimensions that they may be symmetrical in elevation. Parapets or pediments erected in front of attic windows shutting out all prospect therefrom. Rooms designed merely to balance others having to fulfil functions to which the position assigned them is entirely unsuitable. Window openings in city buildings where every gleam of light is valuable to the rooms partly filled with stonework which takes no share of the weight of superstructures. Windows built blind for the sake of uniformity with others, or windows cut across with floors or staircases. Windows made rather of the size and shape, and in the positions dictated by the external appearance aimed at than to fit the sizes and shapes of the rooms.

And again,

In Isaac Ware's 'Complete Body of Architecture', written for students of the art, and published in seventeen hundred and fifty-six, several chapters of the third book are devoted to explaining how a house of this kind should be designed. The author supposes a gentleman with a moderate family to be desirous of building a house in the country 'without columns, or other expensive decorations handsome, though not pompous'. After having laid down exact external measurements for a central block and its wings, Isaac Ware proceeds to the construction and distribution of the various rooms, bearing in mind that it is 'always best to accommodate the inner distribution of a house to the outer aspect when that can conveniently be done'.

Of the design for a house so arrived at Mr Gotch says:

It is evident that the gentleman with the moderate family would have to keep his personal predilections as to aspect, prospect, the relation of rooms, one to another, and matters incidental to comfort, strictly in subjection, in order not to conflict with the proportions and outlines laid down by his architect . . . The left-hand block contains the kitchen, the right-hand the stables. Of the six ground-floor windows in the outlying blocks, the exigencies of internal arrangement require that four should be shams, and it is probable that some of the upper windows followed suit. The route from the kitchen to the dining room lies across a lobby, a room and fifty feet of open arcade before it arrives at the outer wall of the central house wherein the dining room is situated.

When these and other inconveniences are borne in mind, it is manifest that such principles of design could have no lasting vitality.

The aim in such methods was to produce stateliness and dignity. But are not the artificiality of an entablature which displaces the attic windows from their natural position and similar insincerities destructive of dignity? Should we not rather welcome such natural falling into symmetrical form as a building may evince, instead of forcing it where the result would be artificial?

In addition to an intuitive feeling for the symmetrical arrangement of buildings, we have an instinct for uniformity where it is logical and natural. The introduction of variety for its own sake would seem to be almost as dangerous as to try and fit planning to preconceived façades.

That variety which springs from creative faculty and imagination, and is a spontaneous expression of a delight in beauty, or has come from the designer's having something different to express or something he must express better, will generally be delightful; but few things more clearly reveal poverty of imagination than the introduction of variety for its own sake. We shall seldom, if ever, find such variety to have been a good exchange for the quiet and calm which might have resulted from uniformity.

In this and all the foregoing chapters, I have confined myself to houses designed for those who were to live in them. But the problems presented to the designer of houses built to let or sell are very different. In the latter a due expression of the owner's personality has to be weighed against his duty to his neighbours; namely, not to thrust that personality upon them, but to present a quiet restrained exterior to them. In the former, anything striking or noticeable in external appearance is more easily avoided, and the expression of the individuality not left to the interior merely from a sense of fitness but of necessity. The help of a natural symmetry is more likely than ever to come to the aid of the designer, but perhaps the temptation to introduce variety for its own sake will generally speaking prove stronger.

When building houses to let or for sale there is a greater probability that a number will be designed and built together, thus facilitating a more complete and comprehensive architectural scheme.

I have chosen to give here the design for four houses built at Hampstead on Hampstead Way because they form a link between the more personal and individual treatment possible to houses designed for their occupants and the more generalised treatment of those to be let or sold.

Each of these four houses was built by and for its tenant, and the design for each was in its early stages influenced far more by the special requirements and wishes of the individual owner than it was later. One by one the special features of each house were dropped by each client as due consideration was given to the desirable quietness and composure of the external appearance of houses, which were so close together as to be almost in the nature of a terrace. At one stage, in fact, the design for these houses took the form of a row of four, in order that one at any rate of those narrow gaps between houses, which do so much to disfigure our suburban streets, might be

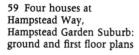

59 Four houses at Hampstead Way, Hampstead Garden Suburb: ground and first floor plans

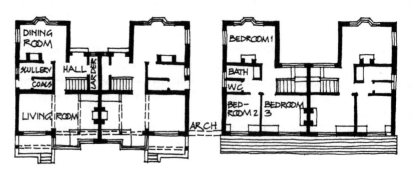

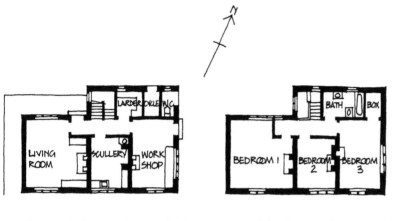

60 House at Croft Lane, Letchworth: ground and first floor plans

avoided, and the comfort and pleasantness of the houses increased. But in this I was not able to carry my clients with me.

The plan for the house in Croft Lane, at Letchworth, has proved to be one of the most economical for a site where the frontage is not so limited as to dictate a squarer form. We should be warned against the too common assumption that the square form of plan is necessarily under all conditions the most economical. It results in a big span of roof, and therefore much space in the roof. If this space can advantageously be made use of, the square plan will generally prove economical, but it so often happens that it cannot be thus used, either because it is not worth the expense and the sacrifice of space on the floor below necessitated by the staircase up to it, or because the required upper floor accommodation can be provided directly over the ground floor without an attic storey.

The greater span of the roof might moreover entail stronger roof timbers, or more expense in walling to carry the roof than would a roof of smaller span suited to a more elongated plan.

A book might easily and advantageously be written upon methods of treating corner plots and designing buildings to turn corners at the junction of two or more streets. Certainly the customary method shown in the diagram [Ill. 61] has been responsible for very much ugliness.

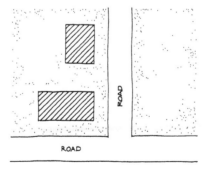

61 Block plan of customary corner arrangement

62 Houses for a corner plot
at Rushby Mead,
Letchworth

When speaking of and illustrating a doctor's house at Bradford, I suggested a little consideration of this point, and again in a doctor's house at Letchworth a way of avoiding the unpleasant results of the customary method of designing for corner plots was suggested.

In two houses in Rushby Mead at Letchworth in which the customary method of turning the corner would have been followed, I was able to secure that the suggestion here illustrated should be carried out. The gain is not only architectural, but each house is pleasantly set back from the road to overlook a little green garden, and all the principal rooms have a south aspect. In addition, some danger to traffic, which exists when buildings come up to a corner, is avoided, for drivers from either direction can see what they will meet when they turn the corner.

15

◇◇

Furnishings Designed to Harmonise with House

Before passing on to other themes I propose to sum up here what has been said in previous chapters in regard to houses designed for occupation by their owners. And in order to do this as graphically as possible, by means of illustrations rather than by abstract theories, I have chosen 'Whirriestone', near Rochdale, Lancashire, as the type of home which exemplifies, more than any other I can call to mind in my own practice, the application of principles of architecture and furnishing for which I have been contending.

'Whirriestone' is, before all else, an expression of its owner's own taste and personality. The disposition and arrangement of the rooms and their accommodation are all her own planning, while the sizes of the rooms are in each instance of her own determining, within a very few inches. Every detail of the house and its furnishing – down to the very handle of the coal box! – has been designed to realise her own clear image of what she wished it to be. And it was in this spirit of intense personal interest and thoughtfulness that all the work was planned and executed.

In the designs for this house I followed my usual custom, preparing slight sketches or perspective drawings for everything before making any working drawings. A few of these sketches are reproduced here to show the method of working. It seems to me that architects would be materially helped in the realisation of what will be the effect of their work in the end, and in their grasp of the final result and feeling of the whole, if they more frequently designed in perspective. The mental effort of taking flat elevations and constructing from them in imagination the finished product, is by no means an easy task; whereas if they could see the ideas realised first 'in the round', this strain on their imagination would be greatly reduced, the final aspect of their designs would be clearer and easier to understand and criticise, and their minds would be freer to receive other impressions.

To return to 'Whirriestone'. It will be seen from the plans that the one good living room or 'houseplace' (which every house should have, however much or little else it has) is especially large. Whatever sunlight there may be during the day will find its way into this room, with the exception of the early morning rays which will come into the study. Further, it will be seen that all the traffic through this room is

103

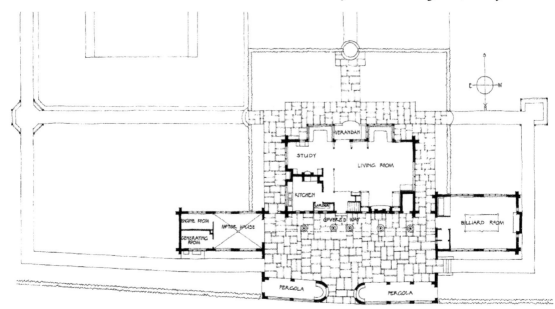

63 'Whirriestone',
Rochdale: ground floor plan

64 'Whirriestone': exterior
from the south showing the
simple symmetry of the
main block and the hint of
the free planning of the
interior in the side
placement of the verandah
doors

across one corner of it only, so that a visitor could at any time be shown into the study without disturbing any members of the family who might be using the living room.

The rooms of this house have the advantage of not being too high. In comparatively small houses, if the rooms are very high there is

65 'Whirriestone': living room interior. All of the furniture was designed specifically for the house. The detailing, particularly of the joinery, has a refinement far removed from the overt mediaevalism of the early houses

66 'Whirriestone': view from the living room into the study with the sliding screen open. The fireplace on the left was intended to provide additional warmth beyond the reach of the ingle fire

always apt to be a feeling that their height is too great to be pleasant in proportion to their width and length. It will be noticed that this danger has been avoided in the present instance by carrying the higher part of the living room up two storeys of running galleries which look down into it along two sides.

Another characteristic of 'Whirriestone' is the fact that as one enters at the front door a pleasant vista through the house and away

67 'Whirriestone': living
room interior. A similar
view to that of Ill. 65 in a
drawing which reveals the
full spatial complexity of
the room. The heraldic
decoration was not carried
out.

to the south is opened up. This arrangement gives a first impression
very different from the oppressive, inhospitable feeling produced by
the blank wall or dark recesses of a hall which usually confront one
upon entering the average home. All the other views and vistas in the
house have been contrived with this idea in mind, and in some cases
to avoid the objection just mentioned they have been lengthened by
means of a window, or terminated by something of interest.

As the pleasantest view is toward the south, the two principal
rooms have been given a southward 'trend' or 'direction'. That is, the
whole arrangement of each room is such that its occupants enjoy the
best available prospect from those portions of the room which they
will most frequently use and those positions which they will most
naturally assume. The principal rooms look away from the road
because this southern aspect affords the most pleasant view; but no
outside elevation of the house is less agreeable to look upon than any
other, and certainly no visitor could determine which to call the back
of the house.

It should be noticed in this connection that above all the elevations
are the natural outcome and expression of the internal planning.
Some points, of course, are pure ornament, but these unmistakably
proclaim themselves as such and could not be mistaken for

68 'Whirriestone': sketch for wardrobes in the principal bedroom. The window looks out onto the double-height area of the living room. The door on the left leads to the staircase. That on the right to a gallery overlooking the living room.

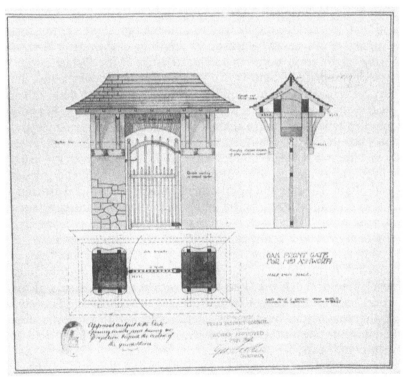

69 'Whirriestone': working drawing for the entrance gateway. As executed the gateway was widened to allow access for motor vehicles after the addition of the motor house and billiard room.

construction, their claim to respect resting solely on the ground of their own beauty. But soundness of construction has never been sacrificed to ornament, and it will be observed that the attempt throughout has been to so beautify the useful and necessary things that they might become objects of interest and decoration instead of being put out of sight and other things substituted. Most of the interest, in fact, comes from construction frankly shown and decoratively treated, the elements and textures belonging to the construction, and the materials used being made the basis for whatever ornament was desired.

It should be pointed out that as far as possible local building traditions have been observed and local building materials used. All the fireplaces are built of stone from the country side; the simple roof is covered with the stone roofing slates characteristic of the locality, and all the stone for the walls, paving steps and hearths was quarried not far from the site.

The general construction and details of 'Whirriestone' are unmistakably, it will be seen, the result of careful thought and individual treatment, all along the most practical lines possible. In fact in all of the houses which I have recently described, the criticism will probably be made that commonsense has been placed before everything else. This would be a somewhat exaggerated accusation, but in a sense it is true. For I do, in a way, put commonsense before everything, believing that the truly artistic is ever the most practical, and that, in architecture as well as other things, if we are not first sensible we can never be artistic, or anything else worth while.

One of the most noticeable characteristics of the 'Whirriestone' interior is the use of 'built-in' furniture. The handy bookshelves, the cosy corner seats and lounges, the cupboards, sideboard, desk – all of these seem and in fact are integral parts of the construction. Not only does this type of furniture achieve a maximum of convenience and space economy with a minimum of housekeeping labour, but it gives to each room a sense of comfort, a home-like quality which the usual movable piece of furniture, no matter how good, can somehow never quite attain. The care and forethought required in the initial planning and executing of each object imply such personal interest, such exercise of individual taste, such ingenuity, and in many cases such originality that the result can hardly be other than sincere.

And not least among the advantages underlying the use of 'built-in' furnishings, is the equally interesting, if unconscious, development of self that keeps pace with the material side of the work. For it is impossible to plan and build and contrive and develop all the possibilities of a home interior without at the same time building up one's inner personality, enlarging one's own field of vision and experience, drawing out unlooked for talents and capacities, and discovering all sorts of novel and delightful channels for self-expression. For the right adjustment of all those intimate little details might make of any dwelling, no matter how humble or how small, a place where every task is pleasant and every corner full of interest, so that housework, instead of being a burden or drudgery, might be a cheerful labour.

16

❖◇❖

Mural Decoration for House Interiors

It is no use attempting to consider the subject of ornament or decoration without first asking ourselves why we ornament; and our attempts to distinguish good ornament from bad will always be unsuccessful if not founded on consideration of the underlying motives. These will be found to be many and various. Most of the finest ornament has been produced because of the desire to honour achievement or to express some great idea, sentiment or principle. It has been an act of worship, an expression of devotion toward some god, or a tribute to the memory of the departed, the recording of tradition, the sacredness of home, to a civic ideal, bravery, hospitality, purity, justice or piety. Much true ornament also has been the spontaneous expression of delight in beauty, in the loveliness of flowers, fruit, foliage, of human and animal shapes, of line, form and colour.

Our debt to symbolism too can scarcely be overestimated. Its use in ornament has been a medium for the voicing of many truths difficult of direct expression. Thus, so long as heraldry was a living art much beautiful ornament grew out of its vitality.

All *true* ornament *must* be the expression of an idea, and what that idea is should be our first concern. If it be a noble one, worthy of our respect, and the ornament in itself beautiful, we should welcome it as a good thing, adding to the joy of life. If we find, however, that the underlying motive is self-aggrandisement, ostentation, display, commercial advancement, personal luxury or the creation of envy in others, then it should receive only our contempt. If we find the purely mechanical and meaningless trying to pass for ornament we should have none of it.

Further, ornament worthy of the name must have given joy to its producer or it cannot in its turn give joy to the beholder; so we may safely reject all which does not bear evidences of the artist's pleasure in making it. For it is not enough to know that the underlying motive was good. The real justification for its existence lies in the fact that it was done with joy.

Browning says 'You may do anything you like in Art, but mustn't do anything you do not like.' This does not mean, of course, that much troublesome, monotonous, painstaking and persevering work will not be involved, but that all such work will be undertaken and carried through gladly, in anticipation of joy in the result.

Judged by these standards what becomes of the patterns machined on most of our wall, floor and furniture coverings, our dress materials, curtains, picture frames, wardrobes and cabinets?

We are better without all that spurious ornament which we find is not in the true sense of the word 'a work of art'. William Morris once said 'Have nothing in your rooms which you do not either know to be useful or believe to be beautiful.' Three tests, therefore, we may always safely apply to anything we purpose to use in decorating our rooms. First we must probe down to the motive for its existence and our use of it; next we must inquire whether it bears the evidences of our own or another's pleasure in its production; and to the third test I shall come later.

Now it is quite possible that ornament may be reproduced by more or less mechanical processes and still give pleasure to the user, but the pleasure taken in producing that which passes through many such processes generally becomes remote before the ornament comes into use and the pleasure the user may derive from it is often very short lived, lessening necessarily in proportion as the processes are mechanised.

Some processes of reproduction involve so much careful thought and so much pleasure in execution, that art is, as it were, kept alive through them. Many branches of the printer's art, such, for example, as wood-block printing of wall-papers and fabrics, and various lithographing and engraving processes, while they enable an article to be multiplied indefinitely, require such exercise of artistic feeling that art is kept alive to the end.

The third test to be applied to anything claiming to be decoration is Owen Jones' time-honoured maxim: 'Ornament construction, do not construct ornament.'

The longer one continues to apply this test, the more one comes to see its truth and to realise what very careful study is needed to find the line of demarcation between ornamented construction and constructed ornament.

Of course, in some cases the insincerity is self-evident. When we see a huge pediment erected over the middle house in a crescent or terrace it is not difficult to recognise constructed ornament, for it obviously adds nothing but expense to that house, and is false in its suggestion that the house is somehow different from or more important than the others.

If we carry up a piece of wall above the roof of a building expressly to form a niche in it instead of forming such niche in one of the walls of the building, we are constructing ornament. If we pile up cabinetwork beyond what is needed for couches or seats, for the holding of our books, papers and clothes, or the performance of other useful functions, or if we design the lines of a chair so that it cannot be constructed in the simplest and most direct way, we are again constructing ornament.

Our three rules must be taken together. If we find the desire is to honour something honourable, to say something worth saying, to express delight in beauty, we shall find this leads us to ornament construction, not to construct ornament, and the pleasure we shall take in our work will make it such as will give pleasure.

To return to interior decoration, not only does its success depend upon its being used to help in expressing such sentiments as hospitality and the welcoming of guests – by dignifying the main entrance, for instance – but there seems an appropriateness in applying it to the fireside, to do honour to the hearth as a symbol of the home. Very much depends upon the decoration being clustered around such given points, instead of being spread evenly, whether sparsely or profusely, or dotted indiscriminately over all surfaces. In a room where many things are equally ornamented, no one piece of decoration 'stands a chance', for its beauties cannot be seen or appreciated.

We need not fear, as we often do, getting a monotonous effect in our rooms, for this rarely happens. When everything possible is done to secure a restful, quiet and harmonious treatment, the people who will come and the things which will be brought into a house will inevitably introduce a greater number of different colours, forms and textures than are artistically desirable, and the last thing which need be feared is monotony.

We can therefore safely have our walls and woodwork one colour throughout the house, and the floors alike throughout. One colour for upholstery and curtains is desirable, for this will generally give an effect of spaciousness, completeness and quiet. We must remember that all these surfaces and hangings are only rightly considered as backgrounds for people and their belongings, such as flowers, books, etc., and their success lies in being effective as such.

Another point to be borne in mind is that to insure that feeling of comfort which is an artistic as well as a practical essential, there must also be a look of cleanliness. Not only must a house be comfortable, but it must look so, and this is impossible unless it looks clean. So the words 'cleanliness' and 'comfort' seem inseparable. It is impossible to get this feeling of cleanliness in a room if the things in it are chosen, like those in the back sitting room of the ordinary boarding house, because they 'will not show the dirt'. To look clean, things must be capable of showing they are clean. If they are of the kind which does not show the dirt, it matters not how spotless they may be, they will never give the feeling of cleanliness.

When speaking of the decorative paintings used in the house at Caterham, I tried to make my position clear in regard to the degree of realism I thought might be permitted in paintings used as decoration. I took a stand for the admission of a greater degree of realism than many would accept. I contended that when an artist leaves his easel-picture, which he has come to consider as a thing apart and detached from all surroundings, and applies himself to decorating a prescribed space, there will probably if perhaps unconsciously come into his work just that element which makes it sufficiently decorative.

And lastly, it must be owned that when all has been said as to other forms of decoration for our rooms, we have to hand in living flowers and plants something in this regard hardly to be equalled and never to be surpassed.

17

Relation of House to Garden

From the architect's point of view the garden is first and foremost a setting for the house. Its main lines should echo, and none should seem to defy or run counter to, those of the building. Some of its vistas should lead up to the house or should be continuations and prolongations of those arranged within it. The garden should, as it were, be an extension of the ground floor plan of the house, adding open-air apartments to those of the interior. It is impossible to conceive the garden plan aright architecturally except as suggested and dictated by the house plan, and both house and garden must be just as much parts of one complete conception as must the ground and roof plans of the house. Just as the house plans must be a logical fulfilment of the conditions laid down by the site, so those of the garden must be the logical fulfilment of the conditions laid down by both site and house. In order to secure unity of result, house and garden should be thought out together as a whole. A garden plan on which the interior arrangement of the house is not shown creates in us the same suspicion of a lack of grasp of essentials as does a house plan which bears no indication of the points of the compass.

All parts of a garden, as of a carpet, should be designed with consideration for their effect from every possible point of view. If they must be seen from certain standpoints, and are a little unsatisfactory when viewed from any other, obviously success has not been attained. Primarily all parts should fall into graceful compositions and pleasing vistas when seen from the windows, or along vistas within the house, or approaching the house. If when looking out of a window one has an uncomfortable desire to move to the right or left or to stand higher or lower, some completeness in the whole has been lost.

One important function of the garden is to bring the house into harmony with its surroundings, to soften the contrast between the rigid and clearly defined lines of the house and the gentle, flowing, undulating freedom of the lines of nature. This cannot be accomplished by attempts to imitate the latter, but by an orderly and logical submission to them.

A garden should be a work of art and should glory in it. As soon as it attempts to appear artless it oversteps the bounds of art. A garden is man's attempt to display and dispose the beauties of plants and flowers in the way best adapted to his own needs and advantage, and the more simply, straightforwardly and honestly he does this, the better. Thus, a path or water channel should take the most direct route from point to point, unless there are obvious reasons why it should do otherwise, in which case very happy results may come from a sweep or deviation. But meaningless windings, wrigglings and meanderings in paths, water-courses or the margins of flower beds and grass plots produce a feeble and unnatural effect.

When it is necessary to secure easy gradients for a drive or path, or a level course for a water channel, or when there is an interruption, such as a growing tree or natural mound, then a sufficient cause is given for whatever change in direction is likely to produce most charm in the result; but we are wrong when we attempt to make what has been *designed* appear as if it had *happened*.

For we never find meaningless lines in nature. The beautiful windings of a natural stream are not the result of chance or whim; there is nothing arbitrary about them; they are just as much the result of fidelity to inexorable laws as are the shape and outline of any chain of hills. They are the outcome of the falls and contours of the land, of the relative density and hardness of different soils and rocks and of many other determining conditions.

A garden may be artless; it may quite happily be a bit of wild nature. And a building may look very well when simply set amidst woodland or moorland, in a copse or field, with no attempt to soften the break between itself and its surroundings. We may even by our encouragement, by our planting and tending of the plants we admire, and by our discouragement of the coarser weeds, assist nature to bring our wild garden to perfection. If, however, we have a planned garden let us see that, like Nature, we have meaning in every line. Let us see that it *is* a garden, a picture, a work of love, not an attempt to deceive or to parody. True art has no converse with deception.

There is a growing tendency to live more and more out of doors, and this the architect should encourage by every means possible. In our English climate the days are comparatively few on which any but the more robust can sit for long absolutely in the open. So varying degrees of protection from the elements have been contrived, such as garden rooms, loggias, stoeps, balconies, verandahs, summer houses, porches, etc. On some days when we cannot sit entirely in the open, the protection of a wall of the house is all that is required to make us comfortable. At other times, in dry weather, we should be quite at ease in a forecourt protected on three sides. In damp weather we could still sit on such a seat as that shown in the sketch for a house at Chapel-en-le-Frith in Derbyshire.

But when thinking out such a house as we should like to have, before making plans we should decide where we shall most value and use opportunities for open-air life – whether on the ground floor or

70 Project for 'A country cottage': detail of porch with protected seating

71 Design for a cottage at Chapel-en-le-Frith, Derbyshire. The conjunction of a sheltered external seat and a bay window with a window seat was frequently used by Parker. This unexecuted design was for Raymond Unwin and his wife, Ethel, Parker's sister. The drawing, by Parker, shows Raymond and Ethel – with their slight height difference greatly exaggerated!

on an upper storey. In the latter case the pleasantness given by a sense of elevation, privacy and aloofness, coupled with the reduced risk of interruptions and intrusion, carries great weight with some people. On the other hand we are lazy creatures and like to have things made very easy for us. If a man can step straight out of his study on to a verandah or balcony and continue his work there, he will do so a dozen times a day; whereas he would remain shut up in his room all the while if, in order to get into the open air, he had to pass out indirectly through the hall. Often the mere provision of permanent seats has converted a little used loggia into a place where some one will almost always be found.

So our arrangements for open-air life must be very accessible, and this constitutes one difficulty in providing them upstairs. Upper rooms are frequently assigned to individual members of a family, either as their bedrooms or studies, so that balconies are limited greatly in their usefulness in that they are usually only accessible from private rooms.

As a rule, therefore, balconies should open out from a landing, though they may also be reached from the rooms.

Open balconies seem to have been very little used where they have been provided in England, although in fair weather it is certainly pleasant to have no roof over one's head.

Even greater protection is afforded when the garden room is formed in the internal angle between two wings of the house, as illustrated by the little sketch given here. It is a great convenience to be able to convert a whole room into a garden room at will by merely sliding back the ample doors into cavities in the walls, and leaving the place open to light and air.

Almost all the accommodation I have been speaking of would be conceded by all as coming properly under the heading of 'the garden' if it were provided in summer houses and garden temples. Tending as I do to place it under the main roof of the house because I find it is more used and more available there, I would still emphasise its garden qualities, and include it in the garden, drawing such line as I do between house and garden at the point at which indoor life may be said to give place to outdoor life.

18

◇-◇

Vistas which Link House and Garden

Possibly the balance of advantages turns in favour of the garden room, for having protection on three sides and being covered-in, it can be used so frequently. Its position on the ground floor also renders it more easily accessible and so more popular than a balcony, and its availability for meals is a great point in its favour. On the other hand many who would be nervous about sleeping in a garden room will have no fear when sleeping on a balcony, and, as I have said before, others value very highly the sense of privacy and elevation a balcony affords. So this question of where open-air facilities should be is one for each home-builder to consider carefully and settle for himself.

I have sometimes heard it argued that these arrangements for outdoor living should be on the north side of a house, on the ground that it is in hot weather one wants to use them, and that therefore places provided for sitting or for taking meals out of doors should be in a shady situation. I, however, regard the provision of loggias, verandahs and balconies from a different point of view, for I look upon them as mainly desirable in proportion to the extent to which they increase opportunities for living in the sunshine and fresh air, rather than as places in which to sit when one would be out of doors in any event.

But the garden room and loggia have another advantage which the architect always appreciates and which the verandah and balcony do not possess; namely, they often help materially in creating those vistas which, being partly within the house and partly within the garden, help so much to link house and garden into unity.

The reader will readily understand this point by glancing at the sketch for the garden at 'St Brighid's', Letchworth. The main vista down the centre of the garden is carried right through the house by means of the garden room with its glass doors opposite to the glass front door, so that on approaching the front door from the north the view through the lobby and garden room, down the garden, meets the eye. Perhaps this advantage in a garden room comes out more clearly in my sketch of the approach to 'Letchworth', Horsted Keynes [see Ill. 43], showing how the trees in the orchard beyond

72 'St Brighid's',
Letchworth: perspective
view showing the
relationship of house to
garden

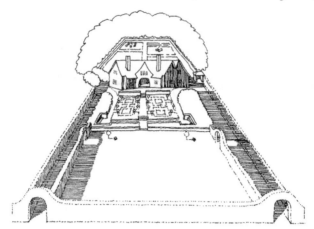

72 'St Brighid's', Letchworth: perspective view showing the relationship of house to garden

are seen through the lobby and garden room, and how these ter-
minate the vista of the approach.

In many instances the gain is considerable if the floor of a verandah
or stoep be extended beyond the area which is under cover. One of
the advantages of having open-air facilities on the ground floor is that
it is more often a simpler matter to carry the floor area beyond the
roofing than it is on an upper floor. Just as some people like part of a
balcony covered and part uncovered, so others like part of a verandah
floor roofed over and part left open. Also where the verandah or
stoep must necessarily be small, its usefulness is considerably
increased by extending the floor out beyond the roof.

In many instances in which economy must be considered,
especially in quite small houses, opportunities for life in the open air
are secured by increasing the various forms of porches or covered
spaces around the doors. But these are not the positions in which
such facilities would be provided from choice, because it is pleasanter
to have them where they will not be intruded upon by every one who
comes to the house. But in the next Chapter I shall show many
smaller houses which have them around the front door, and some
larger ones in which such places are provided at the doors
supplementary to others arranged with greater privacy.

If lily-ponds be introduced, it is important to secure, if possible,
many points of view from above, whence can be seen the beauties of
fountain, tree or flowers, or of a sunset, reflected in the water. For the
value of water in a garden is greatly diminished if there are no points
from which one may look down upon its sparkling, ever-changing
surface.

By designing house and garden together we greatly reduce the risk
of falling into the error of not maintaining a due sense of scale
between the various parts of each. Just as in a square, a place or a
quadrangle or court, success depends on a right relationship between
the size of the enclosed space and the height and proportions of the

buildings which surround it, so in a garden much depends upon the spaces into which it is divided bearing a happy relation to the dimensions and proportions of the house.

Every garden must be divided into a number of sections – outdoor rooms as it were – and the size and scale of each of these must be in pleasant relation to the size and scale of the house and its parts. If a garden presents a single panorama which can be grasped at one view, not only will many charms of mystery and surprise be lost, but also the feeling that the house is at one with and at rest in its surroundings.

The great principle underlying all good design – which is before all things the art of finding that form which best fits a thing to fulfil its purpose – is none the less true of garden design because many of the purposes of a garden are not the most obvious and utilitarian. An important function of a garden is to offer pleasure to its user, and its layout is happiest when it suggests this purpose. Beds which invite us to revel in the loveliness and scent of flowers because they present them simply and accessibly for our enjoyment have something of true hospitality, and walks which seem from their position and form to invite us to an evening stroll have a grace lacking in any which do not manifest a desire to add to our happiness.

We all derive so much enjoyment from the suggestion of *possible* pleasures that it is the business of the garden designer not to neglect this factor in our enjoyment; a successful garden will always owe its achievement partly to its power to invoke at the first glance a lively anticipation of treats in store.

19

Outdoor Life in Porches and Gardens

Realising that the fitness of everything to its purpose is the prime essential to success in gardening as in all other branches of design, it perhaps behoves us to consider a little more closely our purpose in having a garden. From a utilitarian point of view, our object is to secure around the house the air space requisite for health, to grow vegetables and fruit for our table, and flowers which will add beauty to our surroundings and decorate and scent our rooms, and also to ensure a pleasant outlook from our windows so that we shall be less at the mercy of our neighbours in this respect. Moreover, we wish to surround ourselves with pleasant places in which to live and work, rest and play, and entertain our friends. For some of these purposes any form of garden space will suffice, but in other cases the design must be considered.

When planning a garden, let us first humbly search for suggestions from the site, carefully noting the charms it possesses and the sources of those charms, so that if possible we may dispel none of them in the process of translating it from a crude to a finished state. Then let us next assign to everything the place we deem most suitable. Here, for instance, we say, shall be the tennis court, lying with its longest dimension north and south, that the level rays of the morning or evening sun may not shine into the eyes of players. Over there shall be a place for vegetables; yonder shall stand sheltered seats; in other places sunny seats. Fruit trees shall occupy that part, and our favourite flowers this. We will grow hedges here to yield shelter and form backgrounds for our plants and ourselves, and bring scale and proportion into the whole layout. If we do these things with care, and if we put each element of the design where it will come most conveniently, effectively, easily and economically, we shall be also following the path that leads to the most beautiful results. But great stress should be laid upon the logic and economy of our selections. For games such as tennis, croquet or bowls, level lawns of a prescribed size and form are required, so in providing these, many main lines for the garden will at the same time be determined. Some plants require that sunny and yet sheltered places shall be found for them, while others are shade-loving; some again must have sun, but are independent of shelter, while others depend more on shelter than on sunshine. So the form of our garden design will be modified not a little by our choice of plants.

It would seem that the temptation to first conceive an effect for a garden and then sacrifice convenience and everything else to produce it, is less frequently felt than is the temptation to adopt a certain front for a house and then fit in the house plans as well as may be behind it. Perhaps it is more obvious though not more true of a garden than of a house, that it must be the outcome of the conditions laid down by the site. Certainly it is more obvious in the case of a garden than it is with a house that if a design were produced without consideration of the site and the attempt were made to apply it, the result would not be happy.

In most things, true economy brings efficiency, just as surely as true efficiency brings economy, and both give pleasure. Nowhere is this truer than in a garden. The garden in which we feel the site has been made the most of, natural features taken advantage of, local characteristics retained, is the one in which our pleasure will probably be greatest. And it is for this reason that the study of economy is so important.

We have noticed how beauty of ornament, if it is to appeal to us, must be allowed to do so from an ample field of undecorated surface, or at least from a surface of which the decoration has only the value of texture. This is true also of flowers in a garden. We are as dependent on the plain surfaces of lawns, clipped hedges, paving, walling, paths and massed foliage to enable us to see fully the beauty of flowers in a garden, as we are on plain surfaces for the value of ornament on a building.

Great value attaches to these surfaces as backgrounds against which the beauty and delicacy of plants and flowers may be seen to advantage. We are sometimes tempted to substitute, say for a clipped hedge, plants which we think more beautiful in themselves, quite ignoring the fact that these will not make a background for other plants and will not reveal their graces so completely, and therefore that the total effect will be less than if the setting were simpler.

When we have planned the main form and framework of a garden, arranged our vistas and changes of level, and come to the disposition of decorative details, such as ornamental beds and colour schemes, we shall find it best to let these follow and emphasise the main lines and never thwart or contradict them, or seem the result of whim or chance. This will prevent our making the mistake of cutting meaningless angular, circular or shapeless beds in our lawns, destroying that repose and breadth of treatment which are essential characteristics of a lovely garden. Our endeavour must be, in a garden as in everything else, to 'ornament construction and not to construct ornament'.

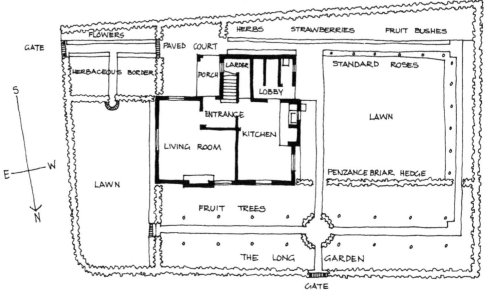

73 Garden plan at
'Brightcot', Letchworth

My plan for the garden at 'Brightcot' in Letchworth is given here as
a typical example of a design for a small garden evolved in the way I
have attempted to describe.

Among the lesser causes of lost charm in a garden it seems to me
one of the most frequent has been the lack of seats. The whole
appearance of the garden is altered by their presence. I would have
them everywhere, terminating and commanding vistas, under banks
and around the boles of trees, but especially close up under the house,
for there they will be most used. Beside the front door seems one of
the most natural positions, partly because it is customary to arrange
some shelter there, and this shelter may so easily be extended to
cover a convenient seat, and partly again because anyone waiting for
a few minutes at the door will not be obliged to stand. For smaller
houses, seats which can be contrived by the front door often have to
suffice. Coming to smaller houses still, one at Megdale in Derbyshire
is given as an example. The porch is here made really almost a garden
room. It commands a magnificent view, is away from the road, is
large enough for meals to be taken in it comfortably, and provides a
fine place for the children to play.

When preparing the design for any cottage I would make one of the
first questions: How far is it practicable to afford shelter around the
door? Consider the average workman's cottage; we could scarcely
find a better instance of how convention, instead of the needs of the
occupants, dictates what shall be provided. If we noted the lives of the
workman and his family what would probably first strike us is the
great proportion of time that is spent at and around the front door.
Here, except in the very worst weather, the housewife spends almost

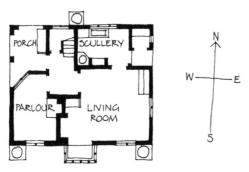

74 Cottage at Megdale, Derbyshire: ground floor plan

every moment of leisure she can snatch; it is the brightest and most cheerful spot she has. Here her husband stands or sits to smoke his pipe in the evening. Around the door is where the children play most. The doorstep is the drawing room of the cottage; all that which corresponds to drawing room life in other circles is enacted there – the equivalent of the afternoon call, the gossip, the friendly chat. The parlour is never used for any of these purposes.

Finally, let me pay a tribute to window boxes. We shall never fully realise what the window box has done toward beautifying many a mean street and keeping hope alive in many a crushed life. Recently in a number of very inexpensive cottages, instead of overhanging the eaves, I expended the money thus saved on window boxes in order to have in a more serviceable form something which would give the invaluable bit of shade lost by doing away with eaves. Not one out of these twenty-two cottages was without plants in the boxes a week after the dwellings were occupied, and the experiment has proved in every way most convincing.

20

Gardens, Open and Enclosed

Before we leave the subject of gardens, we must consider, to speak more accurately, their enclosure. That there must be a fence on every boundary we English seem unthinkingly to accept as inevitable. Even the joy we felt, as children, when we came upon a piece of open road which had not a fence on either side of it, seems not enough to make us pause and ask ourselves 'why', when we propose to erect a fence. When, in other lands, we find tracts of fenceless country, we scarcely realise how much of the beauty of the landscape is due to this absence. Naturally, I have nothing to say against those fences which are rendered desirable by the differences between the systems of farming used here and in other countries.

Roads which should be pleasant, sometimes even in our most wealthy suburbs, are often made almost as dismal as those which pass between rows of unattractive cottages, by the erection of forbidding and unfriendly high fences. The depressing effect of many a row of cottages is more often produced by the fences that enclose the cattle-pen-like front gardens than by any other cause.

But surely the purely aesthetic consideration is a weighty element in this question. Fences cut up the landscape and tend to destroy its breadth and sweep. It is not that fences themselves are necessarily ugly; far from it. What would our pastoral scenes be without the

75 Ground plan of houses at Sollershot, Letchworth, showing open planning of front gardens

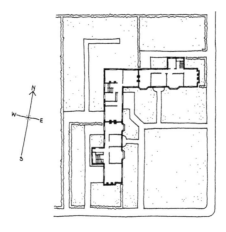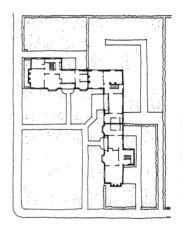

124

hedgerow? Leafy lanes, winding between high hedges, are the glory of our southern counties, and who could contemplate with equanimity the loss of walled gardens? Privacy and seclusion are at times necessary to all of us. Fences are capable of much beauty, both natural and of design, but there is little doubt that our aesthetic sense suffers almost everywhere from the too great profusion of them. The suburbs of many American cities have risen in revolt against the fence and swept it away, with a gain in beauty which has been a revelation to us all. In many of these suburbs each house seems to stand in a lovely open park. But we in England must work tentatively toward this, and not, in the enthusiasm excited by this new idea, lose sight of any real benefits the fence has conferred or can confer.

If we only realised the great number of instances in which a hedge would answer instead of railings or a wall, and acted upon this, we should go a little way in the right direction.

21

$\diamond$

The Court in Domestic Architecture

The progression from gardens to courts, quadrangles and closes is a very natural one, as there is no point where it can be definitely said that one begins and the other ends. English people would gain a great deal in the beauty of their surroundings if they more frequently realised the pleasures the court effect is capable of giving them and were more willing to learn the secrets of the fascinations that a court may hold. In many a tiny space where the attempt to create a garden has been a miserable failure, a court effect of considerable attraction might have been secured. Not that the smallest garden may not be very bewitching, but it is also true that very often tiny gardens which look cramped and seem to draw attention to their own restrictions might have been made to appear almost spacious and to possess a welcoming appearance. As courts they might have some real use, while as misfit gardens no one feels tempted to tread in their diminutive paths or to pause and rest in them a moment. Still, in England we do come across courts possessing the real feeling. Many of the courts and 'quads' of Cambridge and Oxford have it, and the Inns of Court in London are conspicuous examples.

In old-world towns we here and there find a forecourt front garden which has a quiet serenity that even the rushing, hooting motor car seems unable to disturb. Breadth of treatment is demanded in these gardens, and the whole space should be grass grown, flagged or tile paved, except where it is broken by some seat, or fountain or where beds of flowers, from which creepers spring, fringe it. Tubs and boxes with bright green trees in them may be arranged symmetrically, or a flashing pool of water can be in it, like a set jewel. How many of such courts one sees in Italy, France and Germany. The houses of the Levant have almost invariably been built around courts.

In England the court is seldom made the centre of a comparatively small house, yet if it were so it would grant much of the charm that it has bestowed in other ages and bestows in other lands. But if this is to be, the court must not be built, as it is in Italy, to exclude the sun, but so as to 'trap' all the sunlight possible, it must be where we can sit in the open air and sunshine, yet protected from cold winds. We may also have very large doors and windows opening from our rooms upon the court, and these windows may be left open nearly all the time as the court will shelter them from wind and storm. Endless opportunities for through ventilation can be obtained by such a court, and the whole house can be brightened and enlivened by thus bringing the sunlight and fresh air into the very heart of it. Even where the size of the house dictates that such a court shall be very small, it is often amply worth while. The courts in the houses are none of them much more than twelve feet square, yet they are great boons. If a really small house is to be built in such a way as completely to surround a court, it must, of course, be a bungalow. There would not be enough rooms to occupy two floors. In some respects, too, the bungalow form has advantages for such a house, one being that it affords a better opportunity for ample sunlight to reach the court, while the building is high enough to give protection from wind.

To secure the desired court feeling in an enclosed space, it is not necessary that it should be surrounded by buildings on all sides. As I have said, one sometimes finds this effect given to a small front garden even where only one boundary is formed by buildings. Just as by a landscape picture which gives no sense of a 'beyond' or 'way out', an unpleasant shut-in feeling may be conveyed by a court.

Sir Christopher Wren in his great plan for rebuilding London after the fire, adopted a system of dividing the whole area into blocks, each block having a court in the centre, as in the gridiron plans for American towns. Unfortunately, however, there is no evidence that he conceived anything for these beyond the arrangement of show fronts toward the streets, the back elevations toward the courts being left to take care of themselves, and no attempt made to render the courts pleasant or comely. The position held in Wren's time was, that if a front elevation for a building fitted in with the current architectural ideas, it mattered not what unsightliness resulted in the back. Few ideas have been responsible for more ugliness in the world than this, and it is perhaps only recently that we have begun to seriously think about making all sides of a house equally attractive. Perhaps this is easier to accomplish in the buildings around a college quadrangle, which, after all, comprise chiefly one- or two-room tenements, than it is with a number of separate houses around a quadrangle, each with its own scullery, coal place, ash place, baths and lavatories. Still, I can imagine the designer of tenements today claiming that it would be easier to accomplish this with larger houses.

Tenements and flats on the Continent are almost always planned around courts, and working people in Continental towns scarcely know the one-family house. They are housed in tenements almost entirely; eighty per cent of the families in Berlin live in two rooms or one. English working people, on the other hand, almost always have the enormous advantage of living in the one-family cottage. Still, row upon row of these, forming mile after mile of street upon street, have produced district upon district, the dreary monotony of which can

76 Typical working-class
district in an English town

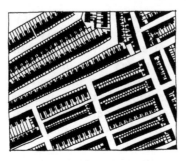

77 Typical working-class
district in a German town

scarcely be equalled. I give here plans of typical working-class sections of German and English towns.

The tenement dwellers in Berlin may be said to have some advantages over the English workingman who lives in one of these rows of cottages, though they are advantages which by no means give compensation for the detraction from family life, and the loss of something more nearly approaching a home which the English workingman may enjoy. The Berliner's dwelling may more frequently be near where he works, preventing the enormous waste of time and energy expended on the daily journeys to and from work. Even if the tenement only looks on to a court, when the occupants have descended the staircase and passed out of the court, they may be at once in a beautiful wide, light street, close to everything, whereas the dweller in a row of cottages might have to traverse miles of the mean streets I have described. Dwellings, even if only tenements, built around a court, have another advantage which in these days of motors is being increasingly appreciated. The court provides a comparatively safe place for children's play, for which the dweller in an English working-class suburb has no equivalent. The children of our work-people have only the street with all its danger, noise and dust as a substitute.

I feel that in the quadrangle of one-family cottages may lie the solution of some of the problems which have been presented, and that by means of this plan we may combine some of the advantages of the English and Continental systems of housing the working classes. I would have swings and sandpits and similar delights in the centre of such quadrangles. There might always be trees and grass and flowers as a substitute for the macadamised expanse of the streets, and the adoption of this idea would lessen the length of the streets required.

Modern motor traffic has by its dust, smell and noise rendered life almost intolerable in a house on a main road, and this alone may compel the consideration of some such plan as I suggest; and the streets would themselves become pleasanter, just as they are in Oxford and Cambridge, from the glimpse into courts the wayfarer has each time he passes an open gateway. But the full consideration of this must be left until the next chapter.

22

◇◇

Comfort and Charm in Small Cottages

The conclusion of the last chapter led us naturally to the subject of the planning of cottages built in rows or in blocks, say, of four or six. This is one of the most difficult problems which architects have to solve. The right course is not to heed the customary methods of solving it, but to take the essential elements of the problem and to disentangle as clearly as possible the requirements and conditions. After studying what has already been done, build up something which will meet and comply with these requirements and conditions. But perhaps the best way of presenting these problems in brief is to show the customary solutions of them and point out wherein these are most conspicuously defective and then suggest ways in which these defects might be remedied. Important as is the question of the aspects of the various rooms in larger houses, it is still more vital when cottages are under consideration, and the time must surely very soon come when it will no longer be regarded as merely desirable that every cottage living room should have a sunny aspect, but it will be considered essential.

The most difficult conditions which are likely to occur are as follows: A plot with very limited frontage on which a detached house is to be placed; a northern outlook of such charm that it must be secured for the principal living room; where a good living room, small parlour, kitchen, scullery, four bedrooms and a bathroom are required, the maximum accommodation likely to be demanded under these circumstances. In cases where the living room must command the view to the north, we may build it to run through from the front to the back of the house, and so meet the demand that even under the most difficult circumstances cottage living rooms must be sunny.

Suppose a builder is asked to erect a large cottage, with parlour and bathroom in addition to the usual living room, scullery and bedrooms. Under present conditions he very naturally will attempt to fit this accommodation to the narrowest frontage possible, and the plan almost invariably produced is some variation of [Ill. 78]. The worst defects in this plan are the back projection which effectually renders the back room and kitchen dismal, sunless and unhealthy, and the unpleasant and wasteful long corridors both upstairs and down. It is not quite so easy to find a plan to substitute for this, which will obviate its worst defects and at the same time comply with the conditions, imaginary and real, which it has been evolved to meet. When the pleasantest outlook is to the south and the road is on the north, there will be some advantage and obvious economy gained by substituting either [Ill. 79 or 80] for this plan. These diagrams cover only about five-sixths of the ground area that [Ill. 78] does, and are conspicuously more compact. The objectionable long back projections have been eliminated, and though we have projections out in front in exchange for them, they are not as saliently objectionable as the back projections, because the only windows which open on to the spaces formed between two of them are secondary windows in rooms which have other windows more advantageously placed. The bright, sunny, healthy open aspect is assigned to the living room. At the same time this room does not lose the much prized outlook on to the road, and has all the healthfulness of a through room, together with light and ease of ventilation; also the parlour may have an east or a west window. The long corridors with their cramped feeling and waste of space have gone. Even if the road passes on the south side, so that the principal window of the living room is north and only its secondary window (the one looking out into the forecourt) is south, surely one of these plans may be substituted for the one shown [Ill. 78] where only the parlour would get a south aspect. As we should always endeavour to provide a through living room in a cottage facing east or west, these plans would have advantages over the other when used where houses have either of these aspects.

That *reductio ad absurdum* in house design, of building from the same cottage plan on different plots, irrespective of any consideration of aspect and prospect, is still far too common to be left uncommented on here. Building bye-laws have done much to secure a minimum air space for all cottages, and our growing knowledge of the importance of sunshine will gradually secure a minimum of sunshine also (in the living room at any rate) for all cottages. The idea that because one side of a house is called the 'back', any degree of squalor is admissible there, and that it may be dismal and depressing, is one which must also gradually lose ground. In the past, people have not only built cottages regardless of their aspect, but have even been known to rent or buy them without knowing what the aspects of the several rooms were.

The backyard has been useful, chiefly as a sort of open-air wash-house. For this purpose it might be retained in many cases, and yet it should be so contrived that it does not form the sole outlook from any window. In several of the plans given here, a sort of a covered yard is shown. In some cases these are large enough to fulfil almost all the useful purposes to which a backyard has been put, together with several others which the uncovered backyard cannot fulfil.

So far, we have only been considering cottages to be built where

78 Bye-law terraced house
plans

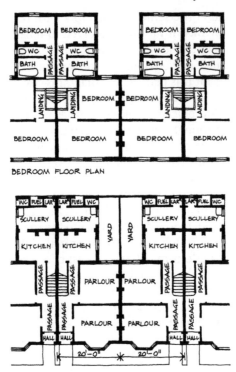

BEDROOM FLOOR PLAN

ROAD

GROUND FLOOR PLAN

79 Alternative terraced
house plans

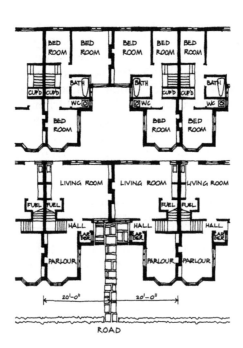

ROAD

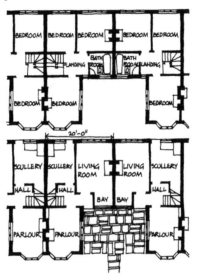

80 Alternative terraced house plans

land is costly, streets and roads expensively made and the frontages therefore the most restricted, and where this limited width of frontage has been allowed to be the chief determining factor in planning. The usual custom in the past has been to plan cottages and the ground on which they are to be built solely with a view to getting the greatest possible number to the acre, and to make any conceivable sacrifice to attain this end. But even the staunchest advocates of this point of view will admit that it only applies to a limited number of areas on which cottages are to be erected, and that there is a growing demand that, even in such places, public opinion and legislation should greatly reduce the maximum number of cottages allowed. This is making it unnecessary to consider the greatly improved type of plan which a larger frontage makes possible. A great impetus in this direction will also be given when the increasing demand for the reduction of the excessive cost of making roads which gives access to cottages, which is prescribed by many bye-laws, has had its effect. In the past, local authorities have found that the easiest way to secure sufficient air space for each cottage has been to demand wide streets, irrespective of the amount of traffic likely to pass over them. The desire to save expense in maintenance has naturally led these authorities to require a high standard in making roads, but they have not foreseen that this would react very detrimentally on the type of cottage which would front on such roads. This is now being widely understood, and also the fact that in order to secure the requisite width between cottages on either side of a road there need not be an equivalent width of street. The space may be provided in gardens for the cottages, greensward at the roadside, or in many other ways. The absurdity of fixing the same minimum width and standard for making streets, whether they were or might be used for important through traffic or only gave access to a few cottages, is becoming patent.

23

◇◇

Planning Groups of Cottages

In the last chapter we considered the building of cottages having narrow frontages; plans for cottages that are less restricted in this respect must now engage our careful study. Perhaps we should begin by considering those which have a frontage not wide enough to preclude their being used within, or very close to, town areas, where land is not so costly that a garden is impossible, and yet is sufficiently valuable to render impracticable anything but a small garden plot for each house – the areas, in fact, on which most cottages are built. In such places the custom is to build the cottages in rows, each cottage as a rule having only the prospect afforded by the row of houses across the street. If the streets run east and west, the living rooms of cottages on the south side face north.

Let us see whether some substitute for the row could not be devised, eliminating some of its most unpleasant characteristics without increasing the frontage required or the cost of building. A photograph of a pair of cottages built at Starbeck in Yorkshire is given here. The design for these cottages was determined by considerations of the possibility of repeating them, arranged as suggested. If the cottages at Starbeck were disposed on the site in the way shown the grave defects of rows on either side of a street would be absent. Each living room would have windows on three sides, and the most limited outlook from any one of these windows would be across two gardens, or one garden and the street. From most points of view a more extended outlook would be commanded. Every living room would have a south window and in addition either an east or west window, and would get a very large proportion of sunshine. Every scullery would face south. Out of every three bedrooms, two would face the south, and the third would have an east or west window, so that an estate laid out on these lines would not have a sunless room upon it.

When laying out an estate on which cottages are to be built, it is necessary in each specific instance to determine first what will prove to be the most economical way of providing access to the back of the cottages. Broadly speaking, there are two alternative ways of doing this, one being by means of back lanes running behind the houses and the other by means of passageways between the houses (one passageway to every two houses). Which of these is more economical can be determined by ascertaining whether the cost of the increased frontage of each pair of houses, caused by the addition of entries between the houses, overbalances the cost of a back road. In [Ill. 82] each back road becomes a front road and additional cost is entailed, but these roads are not essential to the scheme at all. When the cottages are arranged as they are in [Ill. 83] there is no need either to devote frontage to passageways between the houses or to make a back road, and the only way in which the cost would be greater than that of continuous rows would be by the additional end wall required for every pair of cottages, so that it is obvious that a number of cottages could be built more cheaply on this plan than they could in rows. In many instances the expense for drainage would be less. To gain the greatest advantages of either of these suggestions [Ills. 82 and 83] a little covered yard within four walls and under the main roof is especially desirable. Anything in the nature of a backyard or of projecting or detached outbuildings behind the cottages would be overlooked by the windows of other cottages even more than if the cottages were in rows.

It might be well to point out that although this suggestion is put forward as an alternative to rows of cottages and not as an alternative to the customary arrangement of pairs of semi-detached cottages, it may even compare favourably with this infinitely more expensive arrangement, as there is no ugly wasteful gap between each pair of houses and the sun can reach the sides of the houses as well as the fronts. Attention might be called to the fact that with semi-detached houses, in addition to many other defects due to gaps between them, not only are the gaps useless in themselves for garden purposes, but they cause cutting draughts that often render of little value a considerable area of the rest of the garden, front or back. When the arrangement shown is adopted, not only is the whole garden space open to sunshine, but each garden is much more sheltered than it is in any other arrangement. Each is, in fact, almost a walled garden, and very few people will fail to appreciate the abolition of the back road with all that the term implies. Instead of monotonous rows or pairs of houses, with a long line of continuous shade, there would be presented to the passer-by continual change of light and shade, of building and garden; the constant interest of the fresh recesses with variously arranged gardens, revealing themselves one by one; instead of the long strip of sky, wide spaces of cloudland would open to view as each garden opening was reached.

The cottages we are considering may be roughly divided into four main types: those which contain living room, scullery, larder, coal place, lavatory and two bedrooms; those with a third bedroom added to this accommodation; those with working scullery-kitchen and a living room; and lastly the type of building we may call 'parlour cottages'.

81 View of cottages at
Starbeck, near Harrogate

82 Site layout with
staggered arrangement of
cottages

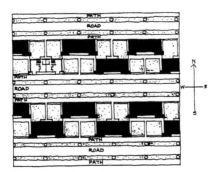

83 Alternative site layout
allowing more economical
use of roads

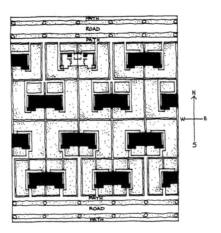

The first type can be planned so as to avoid all projections from the main building, and to attain that cubical form which, because it encloses the greatest amount of space possible to any given quantity of materials, is one of the most economical. [Ill. 84] is given as an example. The second type of cottage at once introduces much greater difficulty in planning, as it is necessary to contrive three rooms over two, all the rooms to be of reasonable size and accessible without wasting space in landings. And the plans must not call for any increase in the ground floor accommodation in order to increase that of the upper floor. When grappling with this sort of problem the architect realises why he should be thankful that the idea of projecting the outbuildings from the main building, or building them quite detached, is being abandoned, for putting them under the main roof increases his available floor area for the bedrooms. [Ill. 85] is given as an example of the second type, designed to be built in pairs.

The types of cottages of which I have spoken may be subdivided again for convenience according to their aspects. But these subdivisions need not be considered in detail. Where the width of frontage assigned to a cottage makes such an arrangement possible, the advantages of having both scullery and living room facing south are obviously great. Efforts should be made to avoid north parlours, as the tomblike impression the parlour will probably give in any case will naturally be increased by a northern exposure. In cottages facing either east or west the ideal living room should run through from front to back, so that, as it does not receive south sunshine, it will get all that comes from both east and west. As a matter of fact, as the sun is lower when in the east and west than when in the south, it penetrates further into the room, and thus the living room will have a greater number of sunshiny hours during the year than if the aspect were due south. Of course, if both parlour and living room are to be through rooms, a very generous allowance of frontage is needed; in most cases this will not be possible. When neither living room nor parlour can be a through room, they should be on different sides, so that one may get the sun at one time of the day and the other at another, the whole house being sunless only a short time each day. It will be noticed that bicycle houses are provided in many of the cottages illustrated here. There are so few cottage homes now where no member possesses a bicycle or a perambulator that it has become essential to provide such a room in most cottages.

This reminds me that when enumerating the uses to which the parlour was put, I overlooked the fact that a very large proportion of them have in recent years established a substantial claim to consideration by housing bicycles and perambulators. But the best argument for the parlour is that its influence, on the whole, has been toward maintaining a demand by the cottage dweller for a higher standard of living. Perhaps the most important thing to bear in mind is that in so far as our efforts tend to raise the standard of the cottage

84 Terraced cottage plans

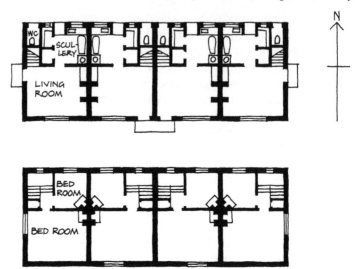

85 Semi-detached cottage
plans

itself and of the cottager's demands with respect to it, the influence
will be for good; that such economies as can be made without loss in
efficiency are for the benefit of the workman and the community, but
all economies made by lowering standards only result in loss to the
community as a whole. Many people are asking for poorer cottages
on the plea that the rents of those provided for labourers are beyond
their means, losing sight of the fact that it is not the wages earned that
determine how good a cottage the workman shall live in, but that the
kind of cottage and style of living he demands determine what his
wages shall be.

If the parlour goes, it should only do so in order to give place to something that will express a truer refinement in the lives of the workman and his family, something demanded by a broadening of their sympathies and tastes, some part of real life exchanged for the attempt to affect supposed symbols of gentility. But until this better thing can be substituted, the parlour should be retained wherever possible without undue sacrifice of realities. The desire for a parlour is but a groping after something better, and symbolises a stage of development which might be hampered if the symbol were taken away.

The time is not very far distant when there will be a bathroom in every cottage as a matter of course. I know it will be truly said if this were done now, a considerable proportion of these bathrooms would never be used for their original purpose, but it is only by providing them that the use and appreciation of them will grow.

24

◇◇

Co-operation in Building and Living

There are many advantages in planning cottages in quadrangular groups. As we have already seen, the arrangement offers pleasant and safer places for children to play in, wider and more cheerful outlooks from windows, and comparative immunity from dust and noise. But this method of planning also makes it possible to obtain architectural effects beyond any that can be gained for cottages in rows, and the utter dreariness of the long row is avoided. Instead of each cottage being the unit of design, the quadrangle as a whole becomes that unit, and the scale is one which offers opportunities for a bigger and broader treatment, capable of a pleasant relationship between the sizes of the buildings and the spaces on to which they front. Cottages built around squares or closes demand no sacrifice in economy of land, and as the space between any cottage and those which come opposite to it on a square is greater than it would be on a street, each cottage becomes more private and less overlooked. This plan also should tend to foster that corporate feeling which is at present so weak and so difficult to nurture among cottage dwellers.

At present the cottager has not begun to realise the economies in time and money which co-operation would win for him, and though his wife would gain even more than he would, she is perhaps further away from it than he. When will people understand that the number of things they may enjoy is practically only limited by their ability to substitute the sharing in great things for the exclusive possession of small things? When will they realise that through the medium of co-operation all may enjoy a share of many advantages, the individual possession of which can only be attained by a few?

Nothing could be more wasteful both in first cost, and expense of maintenance and labour, than the way in which hundreds and thousands of little inefficient coppers are heated on Monday mornings in small, badly equipped sculleries to do insignificant quantities of washing. Here, at least, one would think it possible to take a step in the direction of co-operation. Where cottages are built around quadrangles, how simple it would be to provide a small well-arranged laundry with proper facilities for heating water, plenty of fixed tubs with taps to fill and empty them, properly heated drying rooms, and a children's playroom. The distance from the laundry to

86 Perspective view of a design for a courtyard of 'associated homes' for a site in Brussels

each cottage using it would not be too great, and such laundries would be accessible without passing through a street. As the opportunities which co-operation makes possible come to be realised, the probability is that a boiler would be erected near this common laundry, from which pipes carrying hot water into every cottage would be laid. Common rooms in which to read and entertain friends would be a natural progression along these lines, and some of these quadrangles might even become associated homes, with common dining rooms and kitchens.

But if the average cottager is still far from seeing the advantages of co-operation in this respect, many thinking people of other classes are more alive to it. A large number of these people are seeking the advantages of associated homes, and even co-operative housekeeping; among them are many in those rapidly increasing classes – business women and bachelors who make their home in 'rooms'.

We give here a sketch of some associated homes, for people interested in co-operation, designed for a site in Brussels. In each flat there is a large living room with a bed recess which can be closed off from the main body of the room, a bathroom, a pantry with sink and gas stove in it, a coal place and a lavatory. There is accommodation for bicycles on the ground floor, and each alternate flat on the upper floors has an open balcony. The living room in every flat on the east or west side of the quadrangle, being a through room, gets both east and west sunlight, and has one window looking out into the court and one looking out onto the gardens which surround the whole building. In order to enable the occupant of any flat to go under shelter to the common rooms or to another flat, a cloistered walk runs around the quadrangle on the ground floor. In addition to the flats, the block of buildings contains common room, common dining room and kitchens, and servants' quarters, with accommodation for the manager. There are forty-nine flats. Think for a moment of the economy that can be effected by common cooking alone – of the obvious extravagance of forty-nine separate small households cooking one of forty-nine small dinners on one of forty-nine small ranges, using and washing one of forty-nine sets of pans, when one cook with the help of a kitchen maid and one fire and an efficient cooking apparatus could do the work for all.

At the same time the occupants of a flat need only avail themselves of as much as they choose of the accommodation open to all. They can do such cooking as they like in their own flats, by means of the fireplaces and gas stoves provided there, and may live as isolated a life as they wish. Hot water could be laid to all baths, lavatories and sinks in the flats from the boilers in the central block, and such domestic help as is needed in any of the flats could be provided from the administrative block, at a fixed rate per hour.

Associated homes such as I have been suggesting are scarcely less practicable when they have the accommodation necessary for a family than when they have to meet the requirements of individuals only, as in the Brussels homes. The households which can afford one fire only would not necessarily have it in a cooking range, but could have the comfort of a sitting room fire, and those households which under ordinary conditions would burn two or more fires would probably burn one less.

We must also remember that any system involving material waste stands self-condemned from an economic standpoint. In associated homes for families many further developments of the co-operative principle naturally suggest themselves. Common gardens greater in extent than the area of the quadrangle could be used throughout. Something in the nature of a small hospital, while not only facilitating greater comfort for the sick and more efficient nursing than it is possible in small houses, would also obviate the necessity of each household having its own preparations for illness. Also, the only child, as a member of a larger community, could have some of the benefits that now belong to the child with brothers and sisters.

25

Copartnership Building of Houses

Some people are under the impression that detached houses are in some way more healthful than terrace buildings, even where there are the same number to each acre of land, but I do not think this needs seriously trouble us. The detached houses are certainly colder; they have not the especial advantage possessed by the terrace house, that of compelling the architect to provide for every window an open outlook either across the street or close, or over the garden, while securing the adequate lighting of each room which almost all English bye-laws demand.

In planning terrace houses it should be made possible to get 'a clean blow through' the house, to remove all stagnant air and secure satisfactory ventilation. Almost every room in the detached house can have windows on more than one side, while in the terrace house few rooms can have this advantage, so that satisfactory ventilation is more easily attained in the former than in the latter. This is another reason for claiming that a through living room is almost essential for the ideal terrace house.

Elsewhere I have pointed out the advantage of having all chimney stacks within the house and none on the exterior walls. This, of course, is more easily contrived for houses in terraces than for any other type of building.

But perhaps it is in the garden that the terrace house has the greatest advantage over the detached house. In the plans for terrace houses given in the last chapter, I showed small gardens between the houses and the roads. Whether these are desirable or not depends very largely upon the character of the street on which the houses front. In many streets motor traffic has made it desirable to set the houses back from the street, but where there is little through traffic it is perhaps wisest to build the houses right up to the street line and have the garden on the side away from the street, especially if this is the sunnier side. If the ground between a road and the house fronting on it, instead of being divided up into separate small gardens, is laid out in a continuous strip, as in [Ill. 87], the effect may be most desirable from all points of view, and may help to link a whole road into a single composition.

In order to make clear the advantage the garden of the terrace

87 Co-operative housing
project at Clayton, near
Stoke-on-Trent: site plan

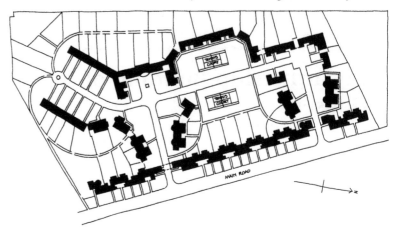

houses possesses, I am here giving plans [Ills. 88 and 89] contrasting terrace and detached houses showing the terrace houses with narrower frontage than those occupied by the detached houses and have given to each the same area of garden. How much more desirable is the form of garden that is possible to the terrace house! The garden for the detached house is necessarily a public and draughty strip around the house, but the garden for the terrace house can be in the convenient and pleasant form of an oblong, secluded from the street and protected from its dust and noises. At the same time, the garden for the terrace houses will be much more sunny and airy and less shaded by buildings, than that of the detached house. The narrower frontage means less cost of land, less expensive road, sewer, gas and water mains, and cheaper maintenance of all these. It also means shorter distances from one house to another, to the doctor, to the shops and places of amusement, and for the tradesmen's daily rounds.

The greater depth in the plots means that the garden site of the terrace in one street is further away from the garden side of the terrace in the street running parallel with it, and is, therefore, less overlooked and more open. Around all our towns we now have a belt of characterless residential suburbs, garish for the well-to-do and drab and monotonous for the poor. Much of the charm of the mediaeval cities arose from the abrupt termination of their closely built streets in open country and the absence of dismal straggling suburban areas. If we should change our ideal of little detached houses each in the centre of its own little plot for something less individualistic, we might come nearer recovering the lost appeal of real street pictures on the one hand and open unspoiled country on the other. The detailed plotting of an area on which houses are to be built should be the result of the most careful consideration of the plans for the houses themselves.

Of late years, however, instead of first planning the houses for the

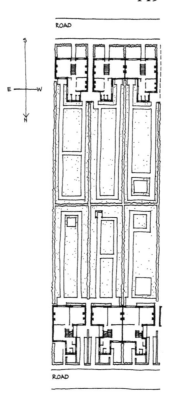

88 Terraced house: site layout

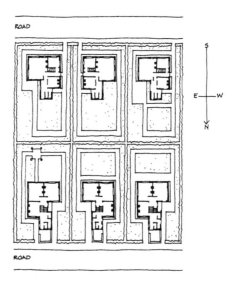

89 Detached house: site layout

different sites and laying out the land in plots to facilitate the best realisation of all the advantages the proposed house plans could offer, land has usually been cut up into plots which were supposed to be suitable for any house. As a rule, the result of this has been that the best could not be made of any type of house plan which was decided upon.

Take the suggestions made here as an instance: These plans were made to meet the objection against providing open spaces, frequently raised, namely that while it would be practicable in many specific instances to furnish the necessary land for an open space, the cost of a road around that open space would be prohibitive, because it could only have houses fronting on one side of it; the other side would have to be left open, as according to the prevailing idea the front of a house must necessarily face the road. [Ills. 90 and 91] suggest that not only may the road be set back and a row of plots for houses planned between the road and the open space, but if the plots on either side of the road be planned to carry out a scheme designed for the houses, without reducing their number, those on the side of the road toward the open space may be so designed as to obstruct little of the view of the open space from those on the other side of the road. Those on the side of the road away from the open space may be arranged so that a greater number can be built, and thus increase the number of those which will have a view out over the space.

Some of the best opportunities for a co-ordinated whole in building are those where the development of land is undertaken by a copartnership tenants society. In these societies the tenant does not own his own house; he owns shares in the society which is the landlord of all the houses comprised in the undertaking. The tenant is not tied to the house he lives in; if it is to his advantage to move to another place, he is free to go, and the responsibility of finding a tenant for his house does not rest with him alone, but with the society as a whole. So long as he chooses to remain in his house, he has all the security that belongs to the man who owns the house he lives in; if he wishes to leave it, he may do so without risk of financial loss. Another advantage is that his money is invested, and his home is situated on an estate which can be planned to the best advantage of each house individually and of all the houses upon it collectively. Such societies have a future far greater than has yet been realised. Their building operations can be undertaken on a big scale, each member sharing the benefits which this makes possible – the standardisation of all the component parts of the buildings and the economies effected by buying in very large quantities.

Copartnership opens up a new range of possibilities, for through this medium all may enjoy a share of many advantages. The wealthy man may have his own tennis court and bowling green and play places for his children, and may secure a wide and pleasant outlook from all his windows, but the man of more moderate means may only have them if he joins a copartnership society. An intelligent land-owner or company may lay out an estate so as to provide for the common enjoyment of some of its advantages, but an estate owned by a copartnership society will naturally be laid out to attain this end.

90 Housing layout, Gidea Park, Essex

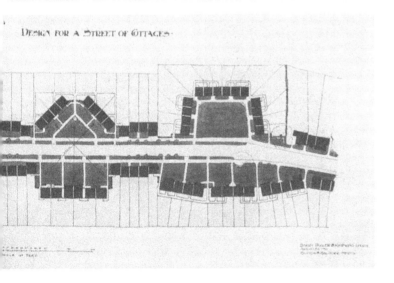

91 'Design for a street of cottages': plan

It will be thought of as a whole; it will be planned for a community; institutes, schools, clubs and common meeting places will be considered; spots of natural beauty will be preserved; distant views will not be shut out; play places and shelters for the children and spaces for outdoor games will be arranged, not only for the enjoyment of these games, but to provide pleasanter outlooks from the windows of the houses, and attractive terminations for streets. The buildings will be designed in groups, not as individual units; these groups taken together will be conceived as larger units, and the whole designed on a big scale. The principle of sharing, therefore, will make each individual house more attractive, the whole scheme being conceived as a coherent and harmonious whole. An organised civic life such as distinguished our old-time villages will spring up and take the place of the ugliness and lack of organisation which characterises buildings produced by the extreme individualism of recent times. It will be the outward expression of the life of a community, taking the place of a mere aggregation of individuals, the hopelessness of which the estate development of recent times has made us far too familiar with.

26

◇◇

Building for Sunlight

I am throughout this book purposely avoiding the discussion of anything which is definitely *town planning*, so far as is possible in dealing with topics so closely related to it. For town planning is too big a subject to be treated as a side issue, and its introduction here would only tend to obscure the points which I have desired to make clear. It is impossible, however, to consider the planning of houses apart from laying out the areas on which they are to be built, just as it is impossible adequately to consider the laying out of areas apart from the planning of houses to be built upon them. But I include only so much about laying out estates as seems necessary to a clear understanding of house-planning problems, this I confine to residential areas.

For some time past the art of laying out such areas has been influenced by two ideals – one, the desire to secure at any cost the largest return for the land-owner, and the ambition to produce certain architectural effects for laying out estates. Our hope for the future of the art is that these ideals shall give way to a desire to produce the right sort of places to *live* in.

In the past, designs have often been influenced by the need of securing good drainage systems and of effecting economies in the amount of cutting and banking required in forming roads. This has led to the layout being adapted to the contour of the land, which in its turn has given rise to a certain naturalness and sanity of planning. But far too often those who have had the work in hand have alone considered how many building plots an estate might be divided into, instead of securing for each plot as many desirable features as possible. In such cases the need of preserving natural beauties has had little weight. Trees have been ruthlessly cut down wherever they presented difficulties in carrying out a plan, and historical associations have too often counted for nothing.

Our consideration then of residential areas leads us to the conclusion that the best chance of arranging them in satisfying architectural compositions lies in aiming to express happy homes made cheerful by sunshine and outlook. The next thing to be considered is the planning of a class of buildings which are best when lit from the north. To this class belong factories, workshops and

92 St Edmundsbury
Weaving Works,
Letchworth: plan

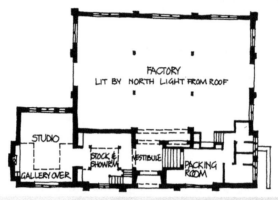

93 St Edmundsbury
Weaving Works: exterior
from the south

studios. But is it really true that all sunlight should be excluded even from the studio and workshop? A steady north light, and any amount of it, is essential, of course, and it should be admitted by windows which face *due* north. If the windows be turned the least bit toward east or west, the worker will be disturbed by the admission of sunlight. But need these be the only windows in the rooms? We must remember that studios and workshops are, after all, living rooms, and that no living room can be healthy if the life-giving rays of the sun never enter it. I believe that such minor windows for the admission of sunlight may be introduced so as not to interfere at all with the proper 'studio lighting' of the rooms, or introduce undesirable 'cross lights' where a north light is required.

A studio and a workshop having such windows are given here, and I am sure no one of the occupants has derived anything but

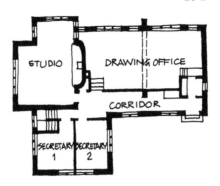

94 Parker and Unwin
Studio, Norton Way South,
Letchworth: plan

benefit from them. If, however, these windows had created difficulties, they could easily have been closed by shutters inside or outside or by a heavy curtain drawn whenever light from that direction was not wanted.

Some people contend that studios and workshops are always best lit from the roof. As a matter of fact, studios which are not exceptionally large may be almost as effectively lit by a big window in the north wall, provided the room is lofty enough to allow the window to be carried up high. For large workshops no lighting has yet been found to equal that from glass in the north slopes of the roofs.

In order to secure such lighting in the weaving works illustrated here, it was thought justifiable to place the building at a slight angle to the surrounding roads. In the case of the studio illustrated here, it was not possible to turn the studio so that any wall came due north, because this room was added to a house that had already been built. My client had suffered from the disadvantages of a studio which had its window facing a few degrees west of north. At the end of the day, when he was pressing forward to finish his work before dark, around came the sun and shone in upon him, so the idea of not having a due north window could not be entertained. However, the arrangement shown here was hit upon as a way out of the difficulty, and has proved entirely satisfactory. Heavy curtains are provided at the west window, so that sunlight can be admitted or excluded at desire, and pure north light may be had when the work demands.

27

❖❖❖❖❖❖❖❖❖❖❖❖❖❖❖❖❖❖❖❖❖❖❖❖❖❖❖❖❖❖❖❖❖❖❖❖❖❖❖

Democracy's Influence on Architecture

I have several times used the expression 'a living art' and it is possible that the exact meaning I want to convey by this phrase is not quite plain. This meaning is clearly defined in Mr Russell Sturgis' delightful book 'How to Judge Architecture', where he carefully differentiates between architecture when it was a living art and that developed out of present conditions. He points out that the art of shipbuilding is alive, even though it might be contended that a dreadnought is inferior as a work of art to an Elizabethan battleship, and might therefore be called decadent. One cannot look on a modern trend as the product of a dead art. If the designer had first to consider whether he should build his ship after a Chinese or Greek or Elizabethan model, it would clearly indicate that shipbuilding was no longer a living art.

Mr Sturgis further deplores the confusing similarity of 'decadent' and 'decaying' and the misconceptions resulting from their mere likeness in sound, and shows that decadent art is not necessarily or even generally decaying art. In the most admirable way he demonstrates that the decadent period in each successive style of architecture began when the essential principles of its construction were lost sight of. For instance, Greek architecture became decadent when the lintel began to be made of small stones; Gothic became decadent when ribs were cut decoratively in the under surface of the vault instead of remaining its vital supports; Renaissance became decadent when columns began to be mere decorations laid on the surface of the walls, instead of being the veritable supports from which the arches sprang to carry the weight of the superstructure and transmit it to the foundations.

We may copy Greek architecture or reproduce perfect Georgian houses or the Gothic form and detail of the village church, but none of these will live again because we cannot revive the spirit of the ages to which they belong – the mythology of the ancients, the religious fervour of the Middle Ages – without which we cannot regain the vital expression of these creations.

If we are to have a living art of architecture again it must be founded on as vital principles as animated these old forms, and spring as inevitably from sincerity, for this is the only basis of what we call

95 Design for a Working Girls' Club in Manchester

96 'The Skittles Inn', Letchworth: interior

originality. It must express the *spirit of the times as its fundamental reason for existence*, though it must do much more than this to become art. The expression of something vital is not enough in itself, any more than the happy arrangement of vistas and terminal features, symmetry and proportion, all the architect's stock in trade, constitute art in architecture. Nineteenth-century art expressed unmistakably its characteristic materialism and mechanical and commercial progress and it was at as low an ebb as art has ever sunk to.

The most vital force in our time seems to be the awakening spirit of democracy, and out of this larger social evolution there are smaller movements, parts or phases of its growth, which are influencing the reconstruction of old forces everywhere to meet its new needs, and it may be that the living art we hope for will be the outcome of this spirit.

As an instance, the prompting of this democracy has influenced legislation in England which enables the aged poor to keep their little homes together instead of being forced, as heretofore, to enter the workhouse or shelter with relatives. This humanitarian law has created a demand for very small cottages suited to the requirements of such people. Planned in small quadrangles, these cottages would give pleasant surroundings and the opportunity for private and quiet enjoyment in declining days.

Democracy's demand for a fuller and more balanced life is further evidenced in the newer architecture in many village communities, where halls for recreation and lectures, and various institutes and clubhouses, are being built to meet the new conditions of social development. These buildings are no longer the bare dismal places that a century ago expressed the democracy's tentative strivings toward ideals, but have grown with its development until now they formulate the higher standards of thought and comfortable living that are significant of advancing conditions.

The accompanying illustrations [Ills 95 and 96] give two examples of the efforts made to fill these demands. These examples but show the trend toward reasonable fulfilment of everyday needs, that may point the way to a living art in architecture again.

It rests partly with the architect but even more with the people to infuse this spirit of democracy into their buildings. The former can help to establish sane and beautiful standards in the planning and construction of houses and public buildings by using his skill for the fulfilment of genuine individual and social needs; but democratic architecture will only be fully realised when the mass of the people take an intelligent interest in these problems and insist upon their dwellings being the sincere expression of their own ideals.

28

◇◇◇

A New Idea in Restoring Old Buildings

The present chapter is devoted to the consideration of an important side of an architect's work: namely, of additions, alterations and repairs to old buildings. The subject will be approached with trepidation by all who appreciate its seriousness, for considerable harm may be done by creating a misconception of his duties in the mind of one entrusted with the repairing of an ancient structure. Misgivings of this nature lead me at the outset to avoid the word 'restoration', lest I might seem to condone much that has been done in its name.

Similar distrust of himself will probably assail the architect who undertakes responsibility for a beautiful historical building. He will realise the significance of the demands made upon him and the importance of his trust. If he happens to be an antiquarian or archaeologist, he may have an uneasy consciousness that archaeological and antiquarian interests are a sign of decadence in any age. He will discover in the work of the artists of any great period no trace of doubt as to the superiority of their work over that of their predecessors, and he will feel how different it is with himself. He must appreciate that he is merely a trustee whose duty it is to hand on to future generations, unimpaired, all the historical interests, the natural and artistic beauties of the building entrusted to his care. And at the same time he must see to it that the work is strong, stable and well adapted to fulfil present requirements.

His task is really more hopeful and perhaps even more wholesome if he is required to render the building constructionally sound while adapting it to fulfil modern demands of comfort and convenience, and not simply to preserve it as a museum specimen whose active life is over.

If he is an architect *per se*, he must necessarily realise that his first business is to determine *what* is beautiful and what is not, and that his next is to decide *why* one thing is beautiful and another ugly. Moreover, he will have discovered that too great an interest in the historical side of his art tends to distract his attention from things of primary importance, and also to weaken his power of design.

It is difficult to formulate rules which may be followed with safety in making repairs and additions to ancient buildings, but possibly the following hints will be found helpful. First, never try to make the new work look old or like the old. Second, never do anything in the new work which falls short of the most beautiful and practical you can conceive, from a mistaken idea of loyalty to the old style or period.

It is good for us sometimes to picture to ourselves what lifeless and meaningless piles our cathedrals and churches would be if their builders, in each succeeding age, had felt obliged to do their part of the work just as the first builders would have done it, instead of each doing what he conceived to be better than his predecessors, and availing himself of his greater knowledge of construction and materials.

In *repairing* a building, our respect for the historical interest of the old work may often lead us to leave parts of it intact and rest content with something that falls short of our modern ideals of beauty and convenience; but in *making additions* to an old structure we must never be hampered in our striving after practical and aesthetic perfection by a fear lest the new work be out of keeping with the old. The most harmonious additions to old buildings always frankly declare themselves such, and often differ from the original entirely in style.

Restorers of one school hold that if they can recover the original design they may reproduce it with no restrictions as to the extent or character of new work used to replace old.

Restorers of another school hold that the slightest repairs to an old building should be done in such a way that any student may discern exactly what is new and what is old.

Without proclaiming allegiance to either school, I would suggest that we should alter old work as little as possible, whenever practicable making necessary modifications in the form of definite *additions*, and never replacing old work with new except where this is constructionally necessary, or where it is requisite to fulfil the purpose of the building, or to insure the health and comfort of those who are to inhabit it. We must remember that we cannot *preserve* the old work by *substituting* new. We should then never replace with new any old decorative features – such, for example, as mouldings that perform no useful function. If we wish for ornament we should add new where none exists; we should direct our efforts toward the preservation, not the replacing of, the old.

To anyone entrusted to work upon an old building, I would commend the most drastic searching of heart, to discover whether or not he is a mere votary of a passing fashion. Let him realise that much which seems to him to possess no beauty may be pronounced by future generations to be the glory of the building he is dealing with. Many of the grossest acts of vandalism in the past have been those dictated by fashion.

Revival follows revival. At one time all the work of the Middle Ages is thought to be barbaric, and public taste cheerfully condones almost

97 King's Langley Priory, Hertfordshire. This shows Parker's skilful integration of new and old building.

any destruction and abuse of it. Then arises a cult, which recognises none of that beauty which springs from symmetry, balance and proportion, and to whom the whole influence of the Renaissance is anathema. At one time the picturesque alone appeals; at another only that which is symmetrical is allowed any claim to be considered as architecture.

He who tends toward such extremes or feels too strongly the influences of certain phases of beauty and is dead to those of other phases is ill-fitted to undertake the care of ancient buildings. Catholicity of taste is necessary. There has always been good and bad taste; it is not simply, as some suppose, a matter of your taste and my taste, both of equal value. Therefore, he who tampers with an old building must be possessed of the ability to see when work is in good taste, even if it makes no appeal to his special temperament. However, it is more usual for an architect to be commissioned to adapt an old building to modern requirements than to repair and leave it to tell its tale of the art, manners and customs of a former age.

King's Langley Priory was little more than a ruin when I was asked to create out of it a new home for an already established school. Part of one of the gatehouses remained and was in use as a shepherd's cottage. Another part of the building was also inhabited, but what is now the drawing room had for long been unused, and seemed never to have been utilised for any but its original purpose, which was probably the stalling of oxen, mules and horses. The beautiful timbered roof was intact though in sad need of most careful repair. New windows had to be cut in the walls and the positions of others changed; chimney stacks had to be strengthened, floors laid, the surrounding soil removed, and new wings were added to give the accommodation required. The necessary staircases were placed so as to interfere as little as possible with the old work, and the outside staircase was erected at the gatehouse with the same thought in mind.

29

<hr />

Altering Country Houses

It falls to few of us, however, to adapt to modern uses a mediaeval priory; a common problem that confronts both architects and home-makers is that of rebuilding and adapting old houses to new needs. Sometimes, when a worthless old house in an old and well-established garden has been acquired, the only plan is to pull down the house and build an entirely new structure upon the old site. In this way the beauty of the old garden can be preserved, with perhaps only a few slight changes that may be necessary to link the new home with its surroundings. The new house may be contrived to fit into the scheme of the grounds and to look at home among the trees, shrubbery, lawn and flower beds of the original scheme.

It happens more frequently, however, that the old house is too valuable to be pulled down, although it may be ugly or inconvenient, or both, and the accommodation provided to meet past requirements most inadequate for the needs of tenants of a later generation. Such a house provides opportunity for the exercise of whatever ingenuity the architect may possess, and may be a source of very fruitful experiment to him who undertakes to alter and adapt the building, to give it a more beautiful form and render the interior more convenient for modern living.

Much of the allurement and picturesqueness of the old towns and villages which afford us such delight is the outcome of a gradual process of alteration, modification, adaptation and addition carried on from age to age. And it is interesting to observe that the result of this process is delightful wherever it has been carried on in the conviction that the new is better than the old. On the other hand, the effect is unsatisfactory only when it indicates scorn or contempt for earlier work, and when it shows evidences of an attempt to simulate rather than to emulate and advance the work of preceding generations.

For these reasons it will be readily appreciated that the adaptation of an old building to meet new requirements involves many-sided problems that demand most painstaking care and consideration from various points of view. An arrangement must be contrived that will suit as admirably as circumstances permit the needs of the new inmates, and while the fatal mistake of creating 'imitation old' must

98 Thornthwaite Old Vicarage, Westmorland: front elevation before reconstruction

99 Thornthwaite Old Vicarage: view after reconstruction

100 Manor Farm, Norton, Letchworth: original plan

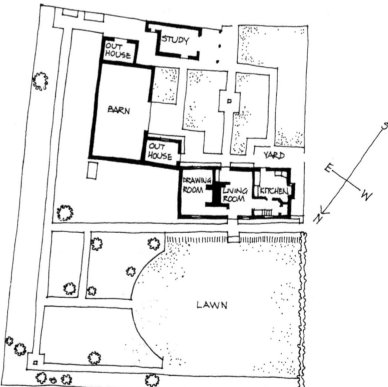

101 Manor Farm, Norton: plan after reconstruction

EAST ELEVATION AS BEFORE ALTERATIONS

GROUND PLAN AS BEFORE ALTERATIONS

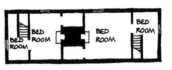

BEDROOM PLAN AS BEFORE ALTERATIONS

102 Cottages at Great Shelford, near Cambridge: plan before conversion

EAST ELEVATION AS FINISHED

WEST ELEVATION AS FINISHED

103 Cottages at Great Shelford: plan after conversion

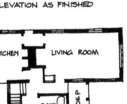

GROUND PLAN AS FINISHED

BEDROOM PLAN AS FINISHED

104 Cottages at Great Shelford: view after reconstruction

be avoided, no charm which the original building may possess should be lost. Perhaps, for instance, the structure to be worked upon has distinction of proportion and emphasis, simple dignity and breadth of effect. These qualities are so easily destroyed that it is only by the most watchful care that they may be preserved.

Notes

Introduction

1 The first of Parker's essays was published in *The Craftsman* in Vol. XVIII, No. 1, April 1910. The series ran with only two breaks, Vol. XIX, No. 3, December 1910, and Vol. XXII, No. 5, August 1912, and concluded with the twenty-ninth essay published in Vol. XXIII, No. 1, October 1912. The essays of February and March 1912 were numbered 22A and 22B and were, in effect, one piece on the design of cottages which had, because of its length, to be divided between two issues. Their titles were 'Comfort and Charm in Small Cottages' and 'Planning Groups of Cottages'.

2 Henry-Russell Hitchcock's *Architecture: Nineteenth and Twentieth Centuries*, Penguin Books, Harmondsworth, 1958, and Nikolaus Pevsner's *Pioneers of Modern Design: From William Morris to Walter Gropius*, Penguin Books, Harmondsworth, 1960 (originally published as *Pioneers of the Modern Movement*, Faber and Faber, London, 1936), both refer to Parker and Unwin only as town planners. In his study of movements in town planning, *The Search for Environment: The Garden City Before and After*, Yale University Press, New Haven, 1966, Walter Creese made the first modern assessment of Parker and Unwin as architects and, more recently, they merit a full chapter in Peter Davey's *Arts and Crafts Architecture*, Architectural Press, London, 1980, Chapter 13, pp. 171–182, although even here the emphasis is upon their planning work. An exhibition of original drawings, 'Barry Parker and Raymond Unwin, Architects', was held at the Architectural Association, London, in 1980. The exhibition catalogue has essays by Nicholas Taylor and Dean Hawkes. The most striking omission is from Hermann Muthesius's *Das Englische Haus* (3 vols.), Wasmuth, Berlin, 1904–5, 1st English edition, *The English House*, Crosby Lockwood Staples, London, 1979. This book presents an extensive review of British domestic architecture and makes reference to Letchworth, but fails to mention Parker and Unwin by name even though the work of many very ordinary and long since forgotten architects gain a place. Unwin's life and work has recently been fully documented by Frank Jackson in *Sir Raymond Unwin: Architect, Planner and Visionary*, A. Zwemmer Ltd, London, 1985.

A Biographical Sketch

1 The date of Wright's birth is disputed in the literature. In *An Autobiography*, Longmans, Green and Co., New York, 1932, Wright himself gives the year as 1869, and this has been widely accepted, but Henry-Russell Hitchcock, 'Wright', *Chamber's Encyclopaedia*, Oxford University Press, New York, 1950, and H. Allen Brooks, *The Prairie School*,

University of Toronto Press, Toronto, 1972, have given the date as 1867 on the authority of members of the Wright family.

2 The work of Wood and Ashbee is described in Davey, *Arts and Crafts Architecture*.

3 James D. Kornwolf's *M. H. Baillie Scott and the Arts and Crafts Movement*, Johns Hopkins Press, Baltimore and London, 1972, is the definitive study of Scott's life and work.

4 Mackintosh studies are dominated by Thomas Howarth's *Charles Rennie Mackintosh and the Modern Movement*, Routledge and Kegan Paul, London, 1st edition 1952, 2nd edition 1977, usefully complemented by Robert Macleod's *Charles Rennie Mackintosh*, Hamlyn, London, 1968, revised edition William Collins and Sons and Co. Ltd, London, 1983. Amongst the many books on Lutyens the best references remain the Memorial Volumes, Christopher Hussey, *The Life of Sir Edwin Lutyens*, and A. S. G. Butler, *The Architecture of Sir Edwin Lutyens*, both Country Life, London, 1950, reprinted Antique Collectors' Guild, Woodbridge, 1984. For the houses which Lutyens built see Lawrence Weaver's *Houses and Gardens by E. L. Lutyens*, Country Life, London, 1913, reprinted Antique Collectors' Guild, Woodbridge, 1981.

5 This quotation is taken from Parker's obituary of Unwin in the *Journal of the Royal Institute of British architects*, 15 July 1940.

6 *Ibid.*

7 Barry Parker and Raymond Unwin, *The Art of Building a Home: A Collection of Lectures and Illustrations*, Longmans, Green and Co., London, New York and Bombay, 1901.

8 This building which, after later extension, eventually became Parker's home is now the First Garden City Museum, Norton Way South, Letchworth, and houses much of the archival material on the early days of the town and Parker and Unwin memorabilia.

9 In the *Transactions of the Town Planning Conference*, held in London on 10–15 October 1910, organised by the Royal Institute of British Architects, Ernest (*sic*) May is listed amongst the members as living at 51 Temple Fortune Hill, Garden Suburb, Hendon, N.W. A thorough discussion of May's work at Frankfurt is given in Nicholas Bullock, 'Housing in Frankfurt, 1925 to 1931, and the New Wohnkultur', *Architectural Review*, Vol. CLXIII, No. 976, June 1978, pp. 335–42.

10 The following extract from Regulation 7 conveys the style of this:

The Company, while desiring to leave as much freedom as possible to designers, draws attention to the following points:

(1) A sunny aspect for living rooms should be secured.

(2) Where outbuildings are used they should be so placed as not to block the outlook from the dwelling-houses or present an objectionable appearance from other dwelling-houses. It will generally be found most successful to design them as part of the main building.

(3) Most buildings in Garden City will be open to view on all sides, and should be treated accordingly, the sides and back being built of materials as good as the front.

(4) The Company do not ask for elaborate elevations; they will be satisfied with simple designs, but attach importance to the proportions of buildings and their parts . . .

11 See Kornwolf, *M. H. Baillie Scott*, p. 302. Here Baillie Scott's drawing for Elmwood Cottages is inscribed by hand, 'Examined and approved subject to . . . June 29, 1905, Barry Parker and Raymond Unwin'.

12 Raymond Unwin, *Town Planning in Practice*, T. Fisher Unwin, London, 1st edition, 1909. The book went into many editions and was translated into both French and German.

13 Creese, *The Search for Environment*, p. 297.

Gustav Stickley, *The Craftsman* and England

1 See John Crosby Freeman, *Forgotten Rebel: Gustav Stickley and His Craftsman Mission Furniture*, Watkins Glen, New York, 1966. Interesting discussions of Stickley's role in the American Arts and Crafts movement are offered by Brooks, *The Prairie School*, pp. 21–3, Kornwolf, *M. H. Baillie Scott*, pp. 356–60 and Davey, *Arts and Crafts Architecture*, pp. 183–5.

2 The first issue appeared in October 1901. The journal was published in Syracuse, New York, until 1906 when, with Vol. X, No. 1, April 1906, it moved to New York City, where it was to remain until its demise after the publication of Vol. XXI, No. 3, December 1916.

3 Gustav Stickley, *Craftsman Homes: Architecture and Furnishings of the American Arts and Crafts Movement*, 2nd edition, Craftsman Publishing Company, New York, 1909; reprinted, Dover Publications, New York, 1979, p. 6.

4 Vol. XXVIII, No. 1, April 1915.

5 Stickley, *Craftsman Homes*, 2nd edition, pp. 1–5.

6 Vol. VII, No. 6, March 1905, pp. 567–70.

7 'Special Furniture Designed for Individual Homes: Illustrated by the Work of C. F. A. Voysey', Vol. XX, No. 5, August 1911, pp. 476–86.

8 Vol. XXIII, No. 1, October 1912, pp. 174–82.

9 'H. P. Berlage, A Creator of Democratic Architecture in Holland', Vol. XXI, No. 4, pp. 412–13; same title, Vol. XXI, No. 5, pp. 547–53.

10 See Brooks, *The Prairie School*, for an account of the careers and work of Purcell and Elmslie.

11 'The Story of the Creation Told in Stone in the Great New Cathedral of Barcelona', by Mildred Stapley, Vol. XXI, No. 5, pp. 465–72.

12 Vol. X, No. 1, April 1906, pp. 3–9; No. 2, May 1906, pp. 143–9; No. 3, June 1906, pp. 352–8; No. 4, July 1906, pp. 507–13.

13 'A Bank Built for Farmers: Louis Sullivan Designs a Building which Marks a New Epoch in American Architecture', Carl K. Bennett, Vol. XV, No. 2, November 1908, pp. 176–85.

14 'A House of Fine Detail that Conforms to the Hillside on Which it is Built', Vol. XII, No. 3, June 1907, pp. 329–35; 'The Trail of Japanese Influence on our Modern Domestic Architecture', Vol. XII, No. 4, July 1907, pp. 446–51; 'The Development of Domestic Architecture on the Pacific Coast', Vol. XIII, No. 4, January 1908, pp. 446–51; 'Some Pasadena Homes Showing Harmony between Structure and Landscape', Vol. XVI, No. 2, May 1909, pp. 216–21; 'Domestic Architecture in the West – California's Contribution in a National Architecture: Its Significance as Shown in the Work of Greene and Greene, Architects', Vol. XXII, No. 5, August 1912, pp. 532–47; 'The House Set upon a Hill: Its Picturesque

Opportunities and Architectural Problems', Vol. XXVI, No. 5, August 1914, pp. 532–9.

15 'A New Architecture in a New Land', Vol. XXII, No. 5, August 1912, pp. 465–73; 'Outdoor Life in California Houses, as Expressed in the New Architecture of Irving J. Gill', Vol. XXIV, No. 4, July 1913, pp. 435–8; 'Talkative Houses: The Story of a New Architecture in the West, Told by the Women's Club Building at La Jolla', Vol. XXVIII, No. 5, August 1915, pp. 448–55; 'The Home of the Future: The New Architecture of the West: Small Houses for a Great Country', by Irving Gill, Vol. XXX, No. 2, May 1916, pp. 140–51.

16 Vol. II, No. 3, June 1902, pp. 105–17.

17 Vol. VIII, No. 6, September 1905, pp. 809–16.

18 Vol. IX, October 1905–March 1906.

19 'Town Planning in Theory and Practice: The Work of Raymond Unwin', by the Editor, Vol. XVII, No. 4, January 1910, pp. 391–401.

20 'Barry Parker: An Architect who Designs Houses as a Whole, and According to Need Rather than Precedent', Vol. XVII, No. 4, January 1910, pp. 409–16.

Material and Meaning in Arts and Crafts Theory

1 Unwin, *Town Planning in Practice*.

2 *Ibid.*, p. 136.

3 M. H. Baillie Scott, *Houses and Gardens*, George Newnes, London, 1906, p. 5.

4 *Ibid.*

5 'Special Furniture Designed for Individual Homes: Illustrated by the Work of C. F. A. Voysey', Vol. XX, No. 5, August 1911, pp. 476–86.

6 Muthesius, *The English House*, p. 37.

7 See Robert Macleod's *Style and Society: Architectural Ideology in Britain, 1835–1914*, RIBA Publications, London, 1971, Chapter 8, pp. 123–36, for a summary of this development.

8 Quoted in *ibid.*, p. 126.

9 Davey, *Arts and Crafts Architecture*, in a chapter called 'The Lost City', pp. 116–38, provides a valuable survey of Arts and Crafts attempts at larger buildings. Parker illustrated his designs for larger buildings in *The Craftsman* articles.

10 Macleod, *Style and Society*, p. 122.

11 Geoffrey Scott, *The Architecture of Humanism: A Study in the History of Taste*, Constable and Co., London, 1914.

12 Muthesius, *The English House*, p. 37.

13 John Ruskin, *The Seven Lamps of Architecture*, first published 1849, Vol. 8: *The Complete Works of John Ruskin* (eds. E. T. Cook and A. Wedderburn) (39 vols.) London, 1903–12, p. 27.

14 William Richard Lethaby, *Architecture, Mysticism and Myth*, London, 1891; reprinted, Architectural Press, London, 1974.

15 'Special Furniture Designed for Individual Homes', Vol. XX, No. 5, August 1911, pp. 476–86.

Parker and Unwin's Houses

1 Parker and Unwin, *The Art of Building a Home*, from the final essay 'The Art of Designing Small Houses and Cottages', p. 112. This is the only essay in the book which is in joint authorship.
2 Baillie Scott, *Houses and Gardens*, p. 80.
3 C. F. A. Voysey, 'Ideas in Things', in T. Raffles Davidson (ed.), *The Arts Connected with Building*, Batsford, London, 1909.
4 The plans of Voysey's 'Broadleys', Baillie Scott's 'Blackwell' and Mackintosh's 'Windyhill' and 'Hill House' published by Muthesius, *The English House* are clear illustrations of this.
5 Unfortunately, as is the case with so many of these houses, the original space has been completely obliterated by subsequent alterations.
6 Parker and Unwin, *The Art of Building a Home*, Introduction, p. v.
7 This was published as Plate 14 in *The Art of Building a Home*.
8 No. 15: 'Furnishings Designed to Harmonise with House', Vol. XX, No. 4, July 1911, pp. 394–405.
9 These drawings and those of many other buildings by Parker and Unwin are in a collection of the North Hertfordshire District Council's First Garden City Museum at Letchworth.
10 All of the later drawings have this new name.
11 Parker and Unwin, *The Art of Building a Home*, Introduction, p. vi.
12 'Special Furniture Designed for Individual Homes', Vol. XX, No. 5, August 1911, pp. 476–86.
13 Pevsner, *Pioneers of Modern Design*, Chapter 6, pp. 148–50.
14 Davey, *Arts and Crafts Architecture*, Chapter 8, pp. 82–96.

Gardens and Non-Domestic Buildings

1 Gertrude Jekyll's career and her association with Lutyens are fully discussed by Jane Brown in *Gardens of a Golden Afternoon*, Allen Lane, London, 1982.
2 Baillie Scott, *Houses and Gardens*.
3 Barry Parker and Raymond Unwin, *Cottages near a Town*, catalogue of works exhibited by Members of the Northern Art Workers' Guild at the City Art Gallery, Manchester, Charlton and Knowles, Manchester, 1903, p. 36.
4 Key references in Unwin's bibliography are: Camillo Sitte, *Der Städtebau nach seinen kunsterlischen Grundsätzen*, C. Graeser and Co., Vienna, 1909; and Herman Josef Stübben, 'Der Bau der Städte in Geschichte und Gegenwart', in *Centralblatt für der Bauverwalting*, Vol. 15, 1895, pp. 105–7, 119–21, 126–9, and *Der Städtebau (Handbuch der Architektur IV. 9)*, A. Kröner, Stuttgart, 1907.
5 Leslie Martin and Lionel March, 'Land Use and Built Forms', *Cambridge Research*, 1967.
6 It is surprising that this conspicuous and noteworthy building never received attention from the contemporary press. A full description of it, the Company that commissioned it and the work of its architect are given in D. M. J. Watson, 'Industry in the Garden City', dissertation for the Architecture Tripos, University of Cambridge, 1976 (unpublished).

7 William Morris, *News from Nowhere*, Chapter 3, first published in serial form in *Commonweal*, January–October 1890.

Postscript

1 Aspects of Unwin's public career are documented in C. P. Evans, 'Raymond Unwin and the Municipalisation of the Garden City', and D. Hawkes, 'Garden Cities and New Methods of Construction: Raymond Unwin's Influence on English Housing Practice, 1919–1939', both in *Transactions of the Martin Centre*, Vol. 1, Cambridge, England, 1976.
2 M. H. Baillie Scott, 'A Suburban House', in *The Studio Yearbook of Decorative Art*, The Studio, London, 1910.

Index

Figures in *italic* refer to pages on which illustrations occur.

For EU product safety concerns, contact us at Calle de José Abascal, 56–1°, 28003 Madrid, Spain or eugpsr@cambridge.org.

www.ingramcontent.com/pod-product-compliance
Ingram Content Group UK Ltd.
Pitfield, Milton Keynes, MK11 3LW, UK
UKHW030902150625
459647UK00021B/2672